T0277606

UNTOLD
TAROT

CAITLÍN MATTHEWS

UNTOLD
TAROT

◉ *The Lost Art of Reading Ancient Tarots* ◉

REDFeather

MIND | BODY | SPIRIT

An Imprint of Schiffer Publishing

DEDICATION

To the memory of Yoav Ben-Dov, 1957–2016.
And for all taromancers who keep faith with the ancient tarot decks.

Quas sunt speculorum vitae

"Red Feather Mind Body Spirit" logo is a registered trademark of Schiffer Publishing, Ltd.
Published by Red Feather Mind, Body, Spirit
An imprint of Schiffer Publishing, Ltd.
4880 Lower Valley Road
Atglen, PA 19310
Phone: (610) 593-1777; Fax: (610) 593-2002
E-mail: Info@schifferbooks.com
Web: www.schifferbooks.com

10 9 8 7 6 5 4 3 2

British Library Cataloguing-in-Publication data is available on request.

ISBN: 978-0-7643-5561-5

Printed in China

CONTENTS

Preface 8

INTRODUCTION: TELLING THE UNTOLD STORY 10
Identifying the Cards 11
A Note on Names 18
Choosing a Tarot 19

1 SPEAKERS OF THE UNTOLD STORY 20
What is Tarot for? 20
A Brief History 21
Gaming or Divining? 26
The Bolognese Evidence 30
The Landscape of Tarot 32
Reading Cartomantically 34

2 THE ELOQUENT TRUMPS 38
The Iconography of the Triumphs 38
The Order of the Trumps 40
The Speaking Trumps 42
Trumps as Indicators 88
Sequential Pairings 88

3 THE TALKATIVE PIPS 90
Suit Origins 90
Approaching the Pips 93
Visual Pip Reading 96
Pip Number Associations 99
Qualities of the Suits 102

Combining Number and Suit Keywords 104

The Cartomantic Pips 108

Working with the Pips 128

Suit Interactions 129

Multiples 130

Spreads with the Pips 131

De Mellet's Pips 131

Three-card Layer 133

Four Aces Spread 134

4 THE CONVERSATIONAL COURTS 136

Origins of the Courts 136

Courts and Suits as People 137

Courts by Keyword and Suit 137

Remembering the Courts 139

Reading the Courts Directionally 140

The Cardinal Virtues in Tarot 142

The Courts and the Cardinal Virtues 145

Where Two Courts Meet 147

5 DIVINING SKILLS FROM EARLIER ERAS 150

The Question: Narrowing the Aperture 150

Basic Skills 152

Blending Cards 155

Reading in Lines 158

Direction of Reading 160

The Line of Cardea and Janus 162

Cross and Passport 164

The Pyramid Spread 166

The Fountain Spread 168

6 THE ART OF DIRECTIONAL READING 170

Significators 170

Mirror Pairs 172

Reading in the Direction of the Significator 173

Messengers of News 174

Which Way do the Card Subjects Face? 178

Tableau Reading 182

Tableau of Twenty-five 183

Card-sifting 190

7 TELLING THE UNKNOWN STORY 194

The Oldest Spreads 194

The Pratesi Sheet Spread 194

Grimpetto's Spread 195

Finding the Way Spread 197

The House of Triumphs Tableau 202

When the Cards Speak 206

Mapping the Landscape Spread 208

Future Voices 215

Endnotes 216

Bibliography 217

Tarots Used in this Book 220

Index 221

About the Author 224

Acknowledgements 224

PREFACE

Ancient tarots fascinate me. My first ever tarot, back in 1969, was a Grimaud *Tarot de Marseille*, which I worked with while I was at drama school in London, before moving on to the *Rider Waite-Smith Tarot,* on which the pip or number cards each had a pictorial image. Since my favorite toy as a child had been a pack of playing cards, I had a great fondness for the patterns of the pips and found the move from pips to pictures oddly irritating; the framing of the pips by specific and suggestive images seemed to circumscribe my reading, restricting possible meanings to a very narrow set of possibilities.

By the turn of the millennium, the meagre supply of tarots that had been available in the mid 20th century had become a veritable flood. While some were well drawn and deeply considered, others were not: many were often slick, photographic or ill-conceived, as more and more designers jumped on the bandwagon of the Mind, Body, Spirit roller coaster of the 1980s and 90s. As Photoshop techniques developed, so the art of tarot began to change for me. Instead of working as windows into other worlds, illustrated cards began to resemble a passive TV screen. Finally, after a period of deep disenchantment, I stopped using modern tarots for many years, only returning to them periodically. Instead, I explored cartomantic oracles, immersing myself in older decks and historic tarots, and returning to the *Tarot de Marseille*. I have not been alone in this return to older tarots: many taromancers have gone the same way, and there is a steady rise in the reproduction of early decks and a few books on how to read the *Marseille* and other historic decks.

I yearned to know how to use these ancient decks practically. Very little textual evidence supports the divinatory reading of tarot cards. Indeed, some tarot historians remain adamant that many ancient decks were used solely for gambling and other competitive games, not for divination at all.[1] However, divinatory methods are persistent; if playing cards were being used for divination as early as the Middle Ages, when the clergy are recorded as inveighing against such a use, then I'm sure that tarot cards were not exempt.

Over the years, I've worked with the cards themselves to hear what they had to say. It is hard to read historic tarots with clarity or understanding today, largely because we do not share a consciousness with people in earlier centuries whose experience of symbol and image was different from our own. However, we don't have to go back in time or read in an archaic way. The clues to reading tarot actually lie within the tarot itself, much as the means of acting, gesturing and speaking Shakespeare's plays lies in his written dialogue: as soon as we immerse ourselves in tarot practice, the hidden clues leap out and manifest themselves once again. While we may not have handbooks from the time of tarot's inception, we still have our common sense.

Over the course of time, tarot has been colonized by many other disciplines – a movement that 18th-century French developments in esoteric thought have fostered. Writers such as Court de Gébelin reimagined a deeply mythical origin and esoteric use of tarot, based largely on France's fascination with the discovery of ancient Egypt, thus fostering a mistaken belief that the tarot originated there.[2] It is now common to encounter taromancers who steer their decks by the dictates of astrology, the wheel of the zodiac, or the Sephiroth of kabbala, as if the tarot were unreadable without this.

Of course, the classical planets and elements have been central to the development of Western Hermeticism, which has claimed tarot for its own, but I have chosen in this book to present methods of reading that ignore these esoteric disciplines and honor the tarot for itself. More recently, at the other end of history, a New Age revulsion against the tarot's powerful images has resulted in a plethora of bland tarotesque packs whose divinatory teeth have been drawn by the simple expedient of removing all potentially disturbing traditional card symbols so that no one can be affronted or disturbed by them. The archetypal images of the tarot provide a world of possibilities, and any tinkering with the cards results in a toothless tarot that has nothing to say about the challenging events of life – a disabling development, considering that most people usually only approach a diviner when experiencing life's upheavals.

Older tarots tend to speak lucidly and frankly about life as it is – they pull no punches but offer windows into the hidden motivations and distressing challenges of life, giving us pathways of possibility.

My aim in this book is to offer several ways of reading historic tarots so that, with practice and the guidance of the cards, you will find your own method of reading both the powerful trumps and the seemingly less important pips in a fluid manner, finding concise meanings. There is a little tarot history along the way, but this is more a book for the taromancer who wants to work practically with these older tarots.

The temptation might be to handle such ancient tarots with ultra-conservatism and historic kid gloves, but I encourage you to use your decks with confidence and with playful concentration. Use them frequently, asking questions that are both needful and well framed, so that the tarot can give you helpful and honest answers. This is where the dialogue between you and your early tarot can begin, and where the untold story will tell you its tale.

Caitlín Matthews, Oxford, April 2017

TELLING THE UNTOLD STORY

✦

This book explores the practical ways in which pre 20th-century tarots with pip or number cards can be read, drawing upon the older cartomantic arts of blending cards, directional reading and other skills, rather than reading each card from a predetermined list of meanings.

Older tarots like the *Tarot de Marseille* are currently enjoying a great renaissance but, for many, pip tarots are like an untold story that everyone has forgotten, because they require the card-reading skills of a different era. In *Untold Tarot*, you will learn to read their untold story for yourself.

For over six hundred years, tarots have been part of the daily life of people in Europe. Wherever Europeans have traveled, the cards have gone with them all over the world, from the Americas to the Orient. Tarots have been widely used for gaming as well as for divination, but in this book we will focus upon how we divine with them. Tarots were once hand-painted for rich patrons such as the 15th-century Visconti family of Milan, Italy. Popular and affordable printing processes finally made tarots accessible to the less wealthy, and they spread over Europe, continuing to be engraved and block-printed. Today, tarots are a mass-market commodity, available in great profusion, each themed around a different topic to appeal to a wide variety of tastes.

After 1910, with the coming of the A.E. Waite and Pamela Coleman Smith deck, the *Rider Waite-Smith Tarot* – now the most popular tarot in the world – tarots began to have illustrated pip or number cards, enabling readers to access the meanings in a more emotional and visual way: this has, in turn, created new, psychological ways of reading tarot. Since the early 20th century, most commercial tarots have followed suit, providing illustrated number cards and changing the way in which tarot is read: it has become more eclectic and removed from its roots.

Before the 20th century, tarots had twenty-two illustrated trumps, sixteen illustrated court cards, and forty pip or number cards which had no picture, merely emblems on them. In effect, *five hundred years of tarot reading has begun to be lost*; this book seeks to remedy that loss and to refocus on the art of reading ancient tarots.

In the first chapter we will explore what a tarot is and view a little of its history. In Chapter 2 we look at the trumps, their background and usage, while in Chapter 3 we outline the pips and explore two major methods of reading pip cards: mixing the suits with the numbers, whereby a profusion of meanings can be gained, and also a cartomantic method for those who prefer to have a more fixed framework for their reading. Chapter 4 looks at the court cards, their derivation and use. Chapter 5 delineates the major skills we need for reading older tarots. Chapter 6 outlines directional reading. Chapter 7 presents some historic methods and helps us to put all the skills together in more ambitious spreads.

In this book you will find ways of reading that enable the cards to be endlessly talkative, telling the story of your question like a landscape.

IDENTIFYING THE CARDS

When you first use early tarots, it takes a while for your eye to distinguish and identify each card quickly and easily. Here, you can look over the identifying features for yourself, with the help of your own tarot.

Trumps

The printing conventions on the cards assigns to trumps Roman numerals from I to XXI, while the pips have Arabic numerals. However, some tarots only show their symbol and not their number. Note that the pips numbered "nine" in some older tarots may differ from modern Roman numerals by being presented as VIIII rather than IX. Here is a quick guide to Roman numerals in the trumps:

1	I	8	VIII	15	XV
2	II	9	IX	16	XVI
3	III	10	X	17	XVII
4	IV	11	XI	18	XVIII
5	V	12	XII	19	XIX
6	VI	13	XIII	20	XX
7	VII	14	XIV	21	XXI

Fool and Death, *Facsimile Italian Renaissance Woodcut Tarocchi*

The only trump card that remains unnamed is generally XIII (Death in *Tarot de Marseille*), while the Fool is named but unnumbered, not because he was regarded as being at zero – a concept that did not permeate historic tarot – but because he was of little account.

Aces

The Ace emblems are characteristically more ornate or different in appearance from their fellow pips:

Emblems of the Aces, *Tarot de Marseille Pierre Madenié 1709*

Ace of Swords is a recognizable straight sword, but the other swords on 2–10 are curved like scimitars.

Ace of Batons is a branch, but the other batons are depicted as bundles of straight sticks.

Ace of Cups looks like a chalice with a little house perched upon it – based on a medieval reliquary or ciborium – but its fellow cups are depicted without this cover, except in the Queen of Cups.

Ace of Deniers is just a larger version of the 2–10 Deniers, and is the only Ace emblem that is not different from its fellows.

Actual numeration on the pip cards was generally a later development, and some early packs do not have any numbers on the pip cards to guide you, so you just have to count how many Swords, Batons, Cups or Deniers are on the card. Some of the cards have distinctive features:

Swords 2, 4, 6 and 8 each have curved scimitars which make the shape of a mandorla or almond, while Swords 3, 5, 7 and 9 each have sets of paired scimitars transected by a single upright sword, and 10 Swords has the sets of paired scimitars with a pair of upright swords crossed together. In *Tarot de Marseille*, the straight swords of 3, 5, 7, 9 and 10 have the blade upright. In the tarot shown below they are bundled together:

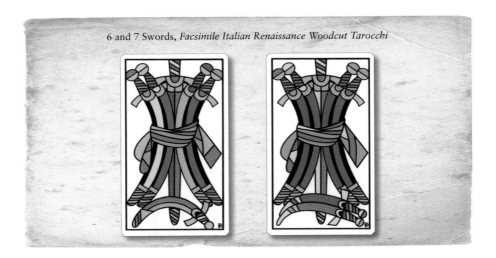

6 and 7 Swords, *Facsimile Italian Renaissance Woodcut Tarocchi*

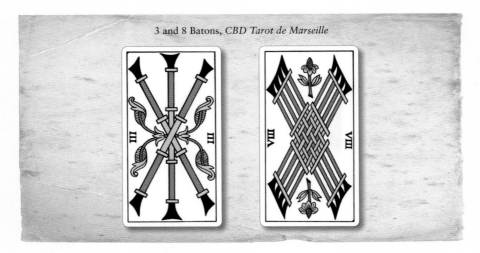

3 and 8 Batons, *CBD Tarot de Marseille*

Batons have straight sticks with dark, thorn-like ends, which cross and interweave on the even-numbered cards. The odd numbers have a single baton centrally penetrating this interweaving. Batons are nearly always straight, unlike the Swords which are curved.

Cups have a golden cup with no cover, except on the Ace and Queen of Cups. The 2 Cups is more decorated, with a pair of dolphin heads, like a fountain arising between the two vessels. Below it is a shield. The 10 Cups shows nine conventionally sized cups, with one huge cup lying with its opening to the

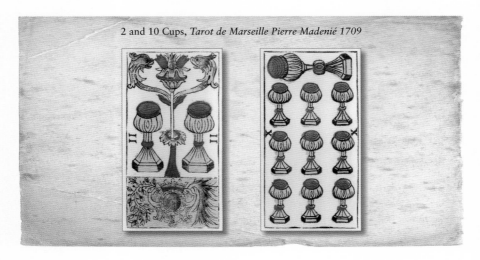

2 and 10 Cups, *Tarot de Marseille Pierre Madenié 1709*

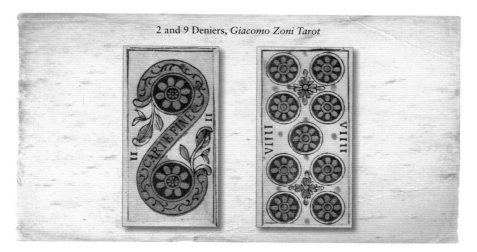

2 and 9 Deniers, *Giacomo Zoni Tarot*

left: within the opening is a four-petalled flower, which echoes the design on the Deniers.

Deniers were coins that were in use in France. They each have the design of a four-petalled flower at their center. The 2 Deniers is traditionally the card on which the *cartier* makes his mark, and there is a banderole scrolling between the two coins with the name of the *cartier* and sometimes the city of origin.

Court cards

Here are the titles of the court cards in French and Italian, so that you can easily identify them:

FRENCH	ITALIAN	ENGLISH
Valet	*Fante*	Page
Cavalier	*Cavale*	Knight
Reyne (Reine)	*Regina*	Queen
Roy (Roi)	*Re*	King

As with modern playing cards, where the court figures are shown in early 16th-century costume, it has been the convention to show the tarot court cards in a slightly anachronistic dress: so, although the *Tarot de Marseille* was made at the end of the 17th century, the costumes depicted are often from the late 16th century.

Each of the courts on the *Tarot de Marseille* can also be identified by their different stances:

Pages stand on the ground, as befitting their serviceable status.
Knights are on horseback, ready to go on a quest or manoeuvres.
Queens are seated, each looking in the direction that her throne faces.
Kings are seated and looking back over their shoulders, except for the King of Batons, who looks forward from his throne.

The courts usually have their own legend under the card image, proclaiming their title.

Queen of Cups and Knight of Deniers, *CBD Tarot de Marseille*

Sword Courts and Justice, *Tarot de Marseille Pierre Madenié 1709*

Within the courts, certain of the figures carry more than one emblem, which can be confusing: the Queen of Cups has a cup *and* a sword-like sceptre, while the Knight of Deniers has a baton in his hands *and* a denier floating before him.

Both the Page and King of Swords have a sword and a sheath. The Queen of Swords should not be confused with Justice. In *Tarot de Marseille*, the Queen faces left, while Justice is one of the five trumps facing outwards.

The Baton courts hold increasingly large batons or sceptres in their hands, with the Page having a log of newly hewn wood, the Knight a roughly hewn club, the Queen a worked sceptre and the King a shortened jousting lance.

The Page of Cups bears a slender goblet, while the Knight has a wider chalice, the Queen holds a covered drinking cup, and the King's cup has a smaller aperture and is uncovered.

Batons Courts, *Vergnano Tarot*

FANTE DI BASTONI   CAVALLO DI BASTONI   DAMA DI BASTONI   RE DI BASTONI

Cups Courts, *CBD Tarot de Marseille*

VALET·DE COUPE   CAVALIER·DE COUPE   REYNE DE COUPE   ROY DE COUPE IIII

Deniers Courts, *Giacomo Zoni Tarot*

The Page of Deniers has two coins, one in his hand and the other at his feet. The Knight has a weapon in his hand but a coin floating before him. The Queen of Deniers holds up her coin, while the King of Deniers has his pointing downwards.

A NOTE ON NAMES

Throughout this book, I have used the following names for the suits (their names in French and Italian appear on page 91):

Swords for Swords
Batons for Wands or Staves
Cups for Cups
Deniers for Coins, Discs or Pentacles

In the trumps, I have largely used the names that appear on the older tarots with which some readers may be less familiar: many of these original titles changed with the introduction of magical ideas at the turn of the 19th–20th century. I will be using:

I Juggler for Magician
II Popess for High Priestess
V Pope for Hierophant
XI Fortitude for Strength

Of course, when we use older tarots, the card of Fortitude goes to position XI, while Justice reverts to its more usual place at VIII.

The division of the tarot into the major and minor arcana didn't happen until 1871, when Paul Christian so termed them in his *Historie de Magie*.[3] Here we will be talking of "trumps" when speaking of the twenty-two cards, "pips" for the forty number cards of 1–10, and "courts" for the royal figures.

Throughout, I have used the term "taromancer" to speak of a tarot reader and "querent" for any client consulting a taromancer. In this, I simply follow the lead of Francesco Piscino, who framed his own convenient word, *tarro-chamente* or "tarotly," in his 1565 tarot treatise.[4] When I refer to playing card divination, I use the word "cartomancy," while for tarot divination I use "taromancy."

CHOOSING A TAROT

To help you study and work with this book, I suggest you obtain a clearly printed *Tarot de Marseille* at the outset – one that isn't cluttered with extra meanings or legends, or other people's interpretations in the margins. If you are used to highly colored illustrated tarots, please adjust your focus: remember, it is not the most ornamented pack that will sustain your learning, but rather the most simple and flexible deck. While you may not understand how to read the pips yet, you will break through and learn how to do so. Although the faces in older packs may be simply rendered, and the color range on the cards appears more restricted than you are used to, there will be at least one tarot that appeals to you. A full list of the tarots illustrating this book can be found on page 220.

CHAPTER 1

SPEAKERS OF THE UNTOLD STORY

✦

And since you know you cannot see yourself
So well as by reflection, I, your glass,
Will modestly discover to yourself
That of yourself which you yet know not of.

WILLIAM SHAKESPEARE, *Julius Caesar*, Act 1, Scene 2

WHAT IS TAROT FOR?

Tarot has been many things at different times: a card game for gambling, a way of poetically complimenting guests at a party, an aid to spellcraft, a method of divination and a means of clarifying your soul. Had we asked this question of people in the 15th century, we would have received some very different answers from any we might collect in a street survey today, when nearly everyone will speak about tarot as "fortune-telling."

Expectations about what tarot is, and how it delivers, have changed from century to century, with the largest upheaval happening in the mid 18th century, with the arrival of an esoteric revolution. This changed things so rapidly that tarot had begun to be seen entirely as a divination device by the early 20th century. By the late 20th century, ever more psychological forms of divination arose, as traditional tarot became more humanist in outlook.

The humanist personalization of tarot has not always held sway. We have only to look at these 15th-century cards, ascribed to Mantegna; these were not so much a tarot as a Neoplatonic representation of the whole universal orders of life, in card form. The fifty cards start with the Primum Mobile of the heavens, working down through the stars, gods, virtues, muses and finally to the estate of humanity, from Emperor to Beggar. Here, humanity features as existing on the lowest rung of the ladder.

In this Renaissance universe, which was already moving from a medieval and Christian viewpoint to a more Neoplatonist outlook, everyone had their own place: people still had a more collective understanding of community and their belonging within it. In our own time and society, we have chosen to see ourselves as self-motivating individuals who owe no allegiances, save where

The Mantegna Cards. Sheet of late 15th-century cards.
Primum Mobile, Saturn, Astrologia, Emperor, Merchant, Beggar

we wish to bestow them, and as the most important inhabitants of the circle of life. As individuals, we tend now to distinguish ourselves as separate from the collective. This evolution of consciousness since the inception of the tarot means that we cannot enter the landscape of tarot as our ancestors would have done: we have largely lost their religious background, their feudal ties of obligation and mindset, and their symbolic imagination. Now, when we approach the reading of historic tarot as 21st century people, we need to appreciate the context of tarot through the viewpoint of its originating consciousness. So, we have to look hard again at what we think we know about tarot.

A BRIEF HISTORY

How did it all begin? This book is not a tarot history, and so what follows here is essentially a very brief overview, yet we cannot leave it out or we won't have a context.

In about 1377 in Italy, there are references to a new game which by the end of the 14th century is called *Trionfi*, or "triumphs." The name "Trionfi," it has been argued, is drawn from the Italian poet Petrarch's allegorical poem *I Trionfi*, begun in 1352, in which Petrarch's own unrequited love for his beloved Laura gives rise to successive triumphal appearances in his long poem. The first triumph shows Love as Cupid, who conquers both gods and men. In the second triumph, Chastity defeats Love, just as Laura herself rejected Petrarch's own advances. In the third triumph, Death defeats Chastity, echoing the fact that Laura died during the Black Death. In the fourth triumph, Fame defeats Death, just as Laura's reputation outlasted her life. In the fifth triumph, Time defeats Fame, while in the sixth, Eternity conquers Time, enabling Petrarch to be reunited with Laura in eternity.[5]

These poetic allegories are somewhat familiar to us, since they feature subjects that appear in the trumps of the Lovers, Death, Chariot, Hermit and the World. However, despite this resonance, none of the great 14th-century Italian writers, Petrarch, Dante nor Boccaccio, mention tarot cards in their works. We will explore these triumphs or trumps further in Chapter 2.

Tarot arises in Northern Italy in the early 15th century, following the introduction in the 14th century of the forerunners of modern playing cards: with the addition of a new suit of trumps, the playing cards were expanded to create the tarot we use today, although it has taken many varied evolutionary paths. One of the earliest tarots comes from Milan and is known generally today as the *Visconti-Sforza Tarot* because it was made for the Dukes of Milan, who were Filippo Maria Visconti and his successor, Francesco Sforza. Actually, fifteen separate decks partially survive from the Visconti-Sforza sets, chief of which are distinguished by their collection names as the *Brera Brambilla* of 1463, the *Cary Yale* of 1445–66, and the *Pierpont-Morgan Bergamo* of 1450–80, made by Bonifacio Bembo. These long, elegant cards were impressively hand-painted and gilded, being used for gaming, not divination.

Carte da Trionfi or Triumph cards appear in the accounts of the Duke of Ferrara in 1442, and there still survive a couple of late 15th-century decks from Ferrara, and some uncut sheets: from these, card-maker Robert Place created his *Facsimile Italian Renaissance Woodcut Tarot*, which is used in this book as an example of a 15th-century Ferrarese deck.

Many wonderful tarots were created in this century, including the earliest surviving complete tarot, the *Sola Busca*, which depicts classical as well as biblical generals and war leaders. It is remarkably different from all other tarots of this time in that each of its pip cards is illustrated – a style of depiction that was not to reappear until the early 20th century with the *Rider Waite-Smith*, which was influenced by it.[6]

Each Northern Italian city-state fostered its own style of tarot and several traditions unfolded over the centuries. The invasion of the French into the Northern Italian city-states in the early 16th century marks the point where tarot developed its own distinctly French variations. It is possible to see, from an uncut sheet found in Milan, that the origins of the *Tarot de Marseille* style of cards began in Italy: this particular sheet shows the Moon with a crayfish, the Star with its kneeling maiden, and the Lightning-struck Tower – all features that are not found in earlier Italian decks but which are very familiar to us from the *Tarot de Marseille*.

The French forerunners of the *Tarot de Marseille* style, seen in the work of Geoffrey Catelin in 1557 and the early 16th-century *Tarot de Paris*, represent a wholly changed set of characteristics: here the Tower trump becomes *La Foudre* or the Lightning, while the Star shows an astronomer with his compasses.

Jean Noblet created what is now regarded as the first of the *Tarot de Marseille* style tarots in 1650, setting the characteristic features we see echoed in most later *Tarots de Marseille*. Other versions followed, with Pierre Madenié of Dijon preparing his deck in 1709, and Nicholas Conver his in 1760–61. A facsimile made by Yves Renaud of the *Pierre Madenié Tarot* is used in this book.

In France, from 1701, card-makers were forbidden to engrave woodblocks themselves, due to new tax regulations. This meant that any previously made woodblocks were seized and burned, ensuring that older designs, so painstakingly carved, were lost to us.[7] To evade this harsh law, card-makers had to call upon engravers to make new blocks that conformed to the new regulations. This is how the details of the Marseille-style decks began to slowly alter: some woodblocks were less expertly carved than others, creating primitive depictions of the figures and making mistakes with some standard features, so that the Hanged Man, instead of hanging from his feet in the customary way, became reversed and was shown upright, like a man with his hands in the air – a feature of the *Viéville Tarot* of 1650. This tarot is of the Flemish style, with characteristics that we recognize from the Ferrara style of tarot, with the astronomer on the Star and the spinning woman on the Moon card.

Political and religious changes wrought their effect upon the tarot in two notable incidents in Belgium and Bologna. The Belgian card-maker François-John Vandenborre (1762–1803) changed the Pope and Popess cards, substituting Bacchus sitting on a barrel for the Pope and the swaggering Captaino Eracasse, a bombastic character from the Commedia dell'arte, for the Popess. Boastful, opportunistic and cowardly, Captaino Eracasse caricatures the Spaniards who policed the Netherlands during its long occupation, showing us what the card-maker thought about such a being as a male or female pope! A facsimile of the *Vandenborre Tarot* illustrates this book. Similar papal discontent was apparent in the *Tarot of Besançon*, a style of tarot used in Switzerland, Germany and eastern France; it arose in 1680, in the wake of the religious wars of the 17th century, replacing the papal trumps with Juno and Jupiter, leading to what is now known as the *IJJ Tarot*.

Meanwhile, in 1725, in Bologna, which was then part of the Papal States, a different kind of papal problem was being played out in a tarocchino pack. Tarocchino, or "a small tarot," was a pack with a reduced number of cards, suitable for playing such games as Ottocento, with only sixty-two cards. One of the earliest of these was made in 1664 by Guiseppe Maria Mitelli, who engraved an elegant *Tarocchino Bolognese*, that which had evolved in Bologna, showing both classical and contemporary Italian images.

In 1725, and following Mitelli's lead, a sacristan named Montieri created a tarocchino pack now generally known as the *Geographica*; in it, he substituted the Four *Moretti* or Moors for the two papal figures and the two imperial figures, so that there would be no offence. These Moors together represented the four continents of Europe, America, Africa and Asia, with the other cards representing different world locations and cities; the very top of each map card bore a minute tarot image so that the player could distinguish its value when they fanned out their cards. So far, so good, but Montieri had unfortunately described the Fool card as *Misto* or "mixed," referring to the government of Bologna, which had both civic and papal oversight. Cardinal Ruffo had Montieri arrested, and a papal bull was promulgated against "vain irregularities and improper ideas" shown in the *Geographica Tarocchino*. The civic authorities finally released Montieri, who was due to be executed over this affair, and for ever afterwards all Bolognese card-makers substituted the four Moretti for the papal and imperial figures, thus creating a wholly new development in *Tarocchino Bolognese*.[8]

Tarots developed not only into smaller packs like the tarocchino but also grew in number, like the Florentine variant, the *Minchiate* decks with ninety-seven cards – it included the usual seventy-eight cards but was expanded by the addition of cards for the twelve zodiacal figures, the four elements, and the three theological virtues of Faith, Hope and Charity. *Minchiate* tarots, also called *Germini* decks, taken from a term meaning "foolish," were in use from the 16th century and, while they remained a largely Italian concern, there also exists the *Minchiate Francesi*, made by the French engraver François de Poilly (1623–93). Between 1650 and 1750, the tradition arose in Italy of depicting the *Fantesce*, or female Pages, on the "round suits" of Cups and Deniers, and showing *Fante*, or male Pages, on the "long suits" of Swords and Batons.[9]

By the late 18th century something truly strange began to happen, probably fuelled by the massive movement of troops during the Napoleonic era: the French *Tarot de Marseille* pattern began to infiltrate the western Italian states of Piedmont and Lombardy, giving rise to what are now regarded as Piedmontese- and Lombardian-style tarots. So, the tarot returned to its land of origin, but in a new form. Two such tarots appear in this book: the *Giacomo Zoni Tarot* of 1789, and the *Vergnano Tarot* of 1830, both reproductions of the originals. Italian tarot makers quickly took up some features of the *Tarot de Marseille*, renaming it with Italian titles, while, in other places, these decks became double-ended, just like playing cards today. This was particularly so in tarocchi or tarock packs, a game that was invented in Germany and took Europe by storm. Using French suits, most tarocchi decks gave up on traditional tarot images altogether, reverting to an array of topics from zoo animals and ballet to imperial tableaux for its illustrations, thus distancing these gaming packs from any previous tarot. Such tarots may have paved the way towards the use of reversed cards, with their double-headed designs.

The rising interest in esoteric matters, which was sweeping France in the late 18th century, fuelled a renewed interest in the *Tarot de Marseille*. While the rest of Europe was playing tarot games, French esotericists such as the Comte de Mellet and Court de Gébelin – who, in his *Le Monde Primitif* of 1781, had suggested both an Egyptian and Gypsy origin for the tarot's images and seen a connection between the Hebrew alphabet and the trumps – were involved in giving the tarot a mysterious and exotic backstory. As a result of their efforts, the *Tarot de Marseille* began to represent a very different kind of movement, where divination, not gaming, became its foremost feature.[10] In the wake of this esoteric uprising, Etteilla, the pseudonym of Jean Baptiste Alliette, created his own esoteric tarot, *The Book of Thoth*, in 1788; now known as *Le Grand Etteilla*, it stands as the first esoteric tarot deck, though it was not to be the last.

The esoteric movement, begun with de Gébelin during the upheaval that led to the French Revolution, continued to fuel France: the works of esotericists such as Eliphas Lévi and Oswald Wirth led in turn to the tarot reaching the shores of England, where it was enthusiastically taken up as part of the curricula of the Hermetic Order of the Golden Dawn, whose initiatory rituals entailed each of its members creating their own tarot for personal use. A.E. Waite and Pamela Coleman Smith, both members of this Order, collaborated to create what is now the most popular tarot in the world, the *Rider Waite-Smith Tarot*, with its fully illustrated suit cards.

Paul Foster Case and others in the United States made their own decks in the 1920s and onward, until by the late 1960s tarot had become big business, but now as a wholly divinatory pack. The rush of tarots that now emerged largely followed the pictorial lead of the *Rider Waite-Smith Tarot*, depicting similarly situated figures and themes. But many decks quickly became thematic, cultural, historic in retrospect, and mythic, while others followed social and spiritual movements to produce tarots aimed at the changing society. Modern and post-modern, quirky, posturing or revolutionary, arty or artless, tarots still keep coming, but now only as divination tools.

We are now in a period that is re-evaluating older tarots that originated before the esoteric movement got under way. Reprints and facsimile reproductions of older tarots are coming out regularly now, and we are indeed fortunate to live at a time when many of the older tarots have been so lovingly restored or re-envisioned, as people often not only want traditional-style tarots but also ones that look more familiar to their time and culture. All over the world, historic tarot interest is burgeoning with many facsimile reproductions and versions of older tarots, like that of the late Yoav Ben-Dov, who re-created the first Israeli *Tarot de Marseille,* and *The Playing Tarot de Marseille* by Ryan Edward, with its playing card suited tarot, which both appear in this book.

However, as interest in historic tarot grows, no one except a few keen gamers is yearning to play tarocchi or any tarot games: people now want to learn how to divine with the older tarots. The information for this skill is sadly thin on the ground, resulting in a recent series of books that have attempted to find a modus operandi for divining with older tarots: Ben-Dov,[11] Elias,[12] Jodorowsky[13] and others have all produced books that seek to explore these skills. So, what is the evidence for early tarot divination?

GAMING OR DIVINING?

It is virtually unbelievable to most taromancers that the predominant use of tarot, from its beginning, has been to play games of hazard rather than divination. Because we live on the other side of the 18th-century watershed, when tarot began its journey towards becoming the main tool of divination, it is hard to fathom how it could have made such an extraordinary transformation.

Playing cards start to appear in the late 14th-century record, before tarot, and are frequently denounced by assorted priests and preachers because people are using them to play games. In 1374, Florence attempted to ban a game called *naibbe,* while in 1379 the Chronicle of Viterbo records: "In this year there was brought to Viterbo, a game of cards, which in the Saracen language is called *nayb.*"[14] This word has clearly originated from *na'ib* or deputy, which is one of the court cards of the *Mamluk* deck, which we will examine later, in Chapter 3 (see page 90). Throughout Europe, from Northern Italy to Germany, France and Spain, we find similar mentions, with civic and ecclesiastical attempts to ban or restrain card games in the late 14th century. Playing cards also spawned lot books, which were early printed books, such as the 1560 *Oracles of Francesco Marcolino da Forli,* which depicts playing cards and meanings which would have been used in a form of bibliomancy, whereby the reader attempted to find the answer to a question. These may be based upon earlier German productions, such as the *Mainzer Kartenlosbuch* of 1505–10, a book that came with short verses denoting the divinatory meaning of each

Sketch from a fresco pertaining to the 15th-century school of Bonifacio Bembo
at Castello di Masnago, Varese, Italy.

playing card. These resemble the kind of moral messages that come out of fortune cookies: "Stop drinking, serve God and live well" or "After a time of sorrow your luck will return."

The visual evidence of tarot being used for gaming in the early centuries is overwhelming: ladies and gentlemen of the Northern Italian courts sit around holding fans of hands, obviously playing cards, in engravings, murals and so on. The sketch above depicts a scene from a mural at Castello di Masnago in Varese in Lombardy, in which three ladies are found sitting in a boat playing tarot; it is evident that they are not divining. Due to the poor state of the mural, it is only possible to make out on the table two cards of Batons and a trump or face card, while the lady on the right is about to lay down 3 Deniers, as she leads a new round of play.

The types of games played with early tarots – Trionfi, Tarocco, Ottocento and many others – are trick-taking games where each card has its own value, higher or lower than the others. One person leads with a card and the other players have to follow suit, if possible, or lay a trump. If you have neither, this is where the Fool, as "the excuse," gets a player out of trouble – he is worth nothing, but he saves you passing out of the game. The trumping and capturing of opponents' cards is followed by adding up the points gained in any trick. *Minchiate* decks were used to play a game with four players, arranged into two teams, just as in bridge today, although it was a very different game. No evidence of *Minchiate* decks being used for any kind of divination has ever been found, though there have been modern attempts to create such a deck.

Tarot could also be used to complement or serve as the basis for a praise poem in a practice called *tarot appropriati*, whereby witty poems could be addressed to friends at social gatherings. For example, here is part of a list of Latin tags cleverly, and perhaps satirically, associating the canons of St Pietro in Bologna with a tarot card, to complement each individual's characteristics:[15]

TAROT CARD	CANON'S NAME	LATIN TAG	TRANSLATION
Mondo (World)	Riccardi	*Microcosmus*	The Microcosm
Saetta (Tower)	Mignani	*Montes conterit*	Mountains wear away
Rota (Wheel)	Conti	*Dives et pauper*	The Rich and the Poor
Forza (Fortitude)	Zambeccari	*Potens in sermone et opera*	Strong in preaching and in work
Amore (Lovers)	Moneta	*Pax vobis*	Peace be to you!
Bagatino (Juggler)	Zanotti	*Laudate Pueri dominum*	Praise our Lord, children!

The last one, for Canon Zanotti, is particularly scathing, since the Juggler has a very low profile, signifying childishness in Bolognese tarot!

The written evidence for tarot divination is very slight indeed, but it is there, recorded largely as a result of civic or clerical disapproval. In *De Rerum Praenotione*, "On the Foreknowledge of Things," written by Francesco Pico della Mirandola to his more famous nephew, Giovanni, in 1507, we discover this passage: "There are many kinds of lots, such as casting bones, throwing dice, and in the figures that are depicted on packs of cards; in the expectation of whatever should arrive first, by choosing the longer stalk, or in casting ones gaze onto a page."[16]

In *A Confessor's Manual* by the Spanish priest Martin de Azpilcueta (1493–1586), which details sins, penances and advice on how to counsel sinners, we read that it is a mortal sin to seek to discover the whereabouts of lost objects oneself, or by asking a diviner, via "lots, dice, cards, books, a sieve or astrolabe."[17] "Cards" could, of course, refer to playing cards, just as much as tarot.

While we seek in vain for more proof of tarot divination, we more often fall over evidence of tarot and playing cards used in rituals and spells. The testimony of a housemaid helped to convict a Venetian woman in 1589: the maid claimed that her mistress, Isabella Bellochio, burned a candle continuously in the kitchen "in front of a devil and the tarots." In her defence, Isabella testified that she didn't light this candle to worship the Devil in any way, but only to cause her errant lover to come back to her. In the same year, a witch named Angela was accused of informing a client that to adore the Devil, she needed to get hold of a tarot pack.[18] Here we have two instances of the tarot fulfilling the need for spell-making.

A similar use in France comes in 1622, when Pierre del'Ancre, the judge appointed by Henri IV to oversee cases of witchcraft in the Basque region of Labourd, wrote his *L'incredulité et mescréance du sortilege plainement convaincue* (*Incredulity and False Belief in that Playing Cards were used by Witches to Seal their Pact with the Devil*). He described cartomancy as "a type of divination certain people practice who take the images and place them in the presence of certain demons or spirits, which they have summoned, so that those images will instruct them on the things that they want to know."[19]

A police record from Marseille tells how, in 1772, two women were condemned to eight days' imprisonment for "taking advantage of the simple-mindedness of several people." Both had taken money in return for cartomantic services that hoped to reveal the whereabouts of stolen or lost things. Another such record relates the punishment of a widow, Anne Cauvin, who on three occasions was to be exposed for an hour in the marketplace wearing a bonnet covered with tarot cards and a sieve around her neck. Afterwards, the tarot cards were to be torn up and the sieve – anciently used for divination – broken.[20]

As we see, these references arise in the context of spellcraft and divination contravening civic laws and offending Church doctrine. They do not speak to us of any cartomantic technique whatsoever. Occasionally, we come upon things like the words written upon the 2 Cups of the late 18th-century Flemish *Vandenborre Tarot*, where we read "*Pour conoistre que la plus basse de deniex et de coupes enporte les plus hautes quand au fair de jeu*" or "Know that the lowest of the Deniers and Cups carries off the higher ones when you play the game," reminding players that, within the Deniers and Cups suits, the lower-numbered cards can beat the higher ones, showing that the deck was intended for playing games rather than divination.

THE BOLOGNESE EVIDENCE

Our best evidence for tarot divination comes from a manuscript page found by Franco Pratesi. This document, now in the University of Bologna, dates from about 1750 and gives a list of meanings for forty-five of the sixty-two *Tarocchino Bolognese* cards, showing that the deck was clearly being used for divination.[21] The date is important, as it is evidence from before the esoteric watershed of the later 18th century. A vestigial method of reading was also found in the Pratesi manuscript (see page 194). Here is the list, with the trumps presented in what we now think of as reverse order, but which is customary in *Tarocchino Bolognese*: note, also, that I have listed only those meanings in the document found by Pratesi, and that several of the trumps are missing, along with many of the pips. Several of these meanings have further evolved in modern tarocchino reading.

We can see how some of these meanings arrived, either because the cards themselves visually suggest meanings, such as the Ace of Deniers for a table, and 10 Cups for roof tiles which the shape of the cups suggests, or because they have local connections for people in Bologna, like the Star, which became associated with the Magi, who are depicted in a 14th-century mural in San Pedronio in Bologna, and so represent a gift. Modern Bolognese decks still show the Three Kings, not the kneeling Star. We also note that the Ace of Cups is "the house," because it shows a tabernacle or reliquary on top of the cup. Some meanings are suggested from the Italian title, so Temperance is given the meaning of "time" because it begins with the same four letters as *tempo*, which is "time" in Italian. No reverse meanings appear. Later 19th-century meanings develop from these ones of 1750, and are still used by Bolognese diviners. Some of these are very strange, with the Chariot now signifying a bed, largely because modern tarocchino decks are often double-headed and the Chariot's body has become immensely elongated into a bed-shaped rectangle. In addition to this early list, there exist several tarocchino packs with handwritten meanings on them from 1820 to 30, from 1860 to 70 and from 1920, showing a consistency of divination, even if some of the meanings have mutated slightly.

We can immediately see that these meanings have arisen from a *visual perception* of the card, each of which today has its alternative divinatory name, so the Knight of Deniers is also known as *l'Ambasciata* or "the Ambassador," who can show up as a negotiator, while 10 Cups becomes *Fiorimento* or "increase" and can denote the flow of blood. The explicit X-shape of 8 Batons

Opposite: The Pratesi document of meanings for
the *Tarocchino Bolognese* cards from 1750

CARD TITLE	DIVINATORY MEANING
Trumps	
Angelo/Angel or Judgement	A wedding, a settlement
Mondo/World	A long journey
Sole/Sun	Day
Luna/Moon	Night
Stella/Star	Gift
Diavolo/Devil	Rage
Morte/Death	Death
Traditore/Hanged Man	Betrayal
Vecchio/Hermit	Old man
Forza/Fortitude	Violence
Tempra/Temperance	Time
Carro/Chariot	A journey
Amore/Lovers	Love
Begato/Juggler	Married man
Matto/Fool	Madness
Batons	
Re/King	An unmarried gentleman
Regina/Queen	A whore
Cavallo/Knight	Door-knocker
Fante/Page	The thoughts of a lady
Asso/Ace	A noble
Cups	
Re/King	An old man
Regina/Queen	A married lady
Cavallo/Knight	Settlement/agreement
Fante/Page	The (young) lady
Asso/Ace	The house
Dieci/Ten	Roof tiles
Swords	
Re/King	An evil tongue
Dieci/Ten	Tears
Asso/Ace	Letter
Deniers	
Re/King	The man
Regina/Queen	Truth
Cavallo/Knight	Thoughts of the man
Fante/Page	Young lady
Asso/Ace	Table
Dieci/Ten	Money

is seen as *La Strada*, or "the street," because it looks like a crossroads. This is the street style of a taromancer who relies upon a visual understanding of the card, rather than a learned set of rules, giving each card a name associated with its meaning. This is how cartomancy arose, by visual association and street wisdom, passed down from one diviner to another.

We should be aware that such visually associated meanings arise within the context of their times and will shift meaning as society evolves. In modern taromancy, the Hanged Man no longer signifies capital punishment in most civilized countries. Recent meanings have elided into the vaguer "sacrifice" or "spiritual attainment," associating the image with the Norse myth of Odin hanging on a tree in pursuit of knowledge whereas, for medieval Italians, the Hanged Man was a malefactor and traitor. Time and distance change things.

Another document, recorded in a disquisition on Bolognese cartomancy by Bruno Mengoli, who belonged to a noted family of puppeteers, speaks of someone called Grimpetto, who lived in Bologna in 1730. (See page 195 for a spread attributed to him.) No further information has been discovered about this character, whom Mengoli reports as "a learned expert in the popular traditions of Bologna's citizens."[22]

So, the question remains: How can we read older tarots in ways that respect the tarot, while at the same time ignoring those games which many tarot historians see as the primary use of a tarot? Follow me as we find out.

THE LANDSCAPE OF TAROT

In this book, I will be focusing on tarot as a means of divinatory storytelling so that we can locate ourselves in the landscape of our lives. The word "landscape" first came into the English language from the Netherlands, where landscape painting had developed from the Middle Ages onwards, revealing homes and activities framed by distant hills, farmland and townscapes. In Dutch, *landskip* just meant "the state or shape of the land." But while this translated into 17th-century English as "a picture representing natural scenery," by the 18th century its meaning had become "a view or prospect of natural inland scenery, that can be taken in, at a glance, from one point of view." Remember that definition!

Tarot offers us a landscape that is related to the perceptions beyond the eye. It both reflects and refracts, giving and receiving at the same time. While our eyes see its appearances, our understanding relates to symbols that are reflected within these appearances. These deeper meanings call out to a body of lore that is culturally received and mythically encoded in us, accessible to our imaginal perception. Which is why, when we visit a piece of land, we don't just see its physical features as "a beauty spot," but also apprehend its essence as a profound expression of that region, with all its historical or cultural associations.

So, when we regard a tarot spread – which is really "a view at one glance" of the landscape of a querent's situation – we discover features that are reflective and refractive. The physical pasteboard cards, their subjects and their relationship to each other meld together like land features, while the querent's question helps to reveal an *inscape,* as the poet Gerard Manley Hopkins called it. "Inscape" is a concept that Hopkins borrowed from the philosophical ideas of Duns Scotus, whereby things uniquely enact their identity.

Each of the tarot's seventy-eight cards is similarly unique, revealing a different refraction of a larger pattern. The way in which the appearance of each card links with its inscape is precisely where we understand its unique quality, giving us the point from which we divine. When several of these cards are laid together, like a storyboard, a distinctive landscape is revealed in relation to the querent's question or concern, allowing the cards to reflect the querent's situation and to refract understanding.

In traditional Australian Aboriginal painting, the images show not only landscape or places to find food, but they are also regarded as visual depictions of caches of wisdom. Aboriginal elders are reluctant to discuss what each of these caches denotes, partially out of respect for the totality of that wisdom, and also so as not to disclose it to those who do not regard this wisdom with similar respect. Only certain elders may be aware of these caches: a view which would correspond to our modern esoteric view of the tarot as a map of the spiritual universe, as it is often referenced by tarot's associations with kabbala or astrology. Of course, on a more immediate level, Aboriginals see their paintings not just as conveyers of abstract concepts but as maps of *the actual landscape* through which they are really walking, whereby each land feature comes with its own totality of traditions and stories: this view corresponds to a more cartomantic and essentially pragmatic way of reading the cards, which we are going to be using here.

Tarot has been revealing the landscape of itself in similar ways. Although people now alive may have lost or never known the older ways of using tarot, it is by working with it that we suddenly access a whole new landscape whose wisdom shows us where we are. Tarot cards can be meaningful as single cards or in certain combinations but, taken together with a question, they create a landscape that allows us to see the context. By laying out tarot cards, we see how they embody the landscape through which we are walking, making the cube of space and time through which we pass appreciable, as the trumps, courts and pips stop being separate entities, becoming instead speakers of wisdom.

Tarot is a craft: when you set out to learn this skill, you look to the hands and words of the master for guidance, but finally you read for yourself, noting the signs that turn up again and again. This is how each taromancer learns to read tarot for him- or herself.

But how do we find that "prospect that can be taken in, at a glance, from one point of view"? By themselves, tarot cards are random, unspeaking pieces of pasteboard. But when they are laid out in response to a question, the whole universe focuses upon the aperture that they make: we suddenly "see" the answer. That diviners can read cards isn't a matter of "belief in" the tarot, but in the simple reading of the signs. In daily life, if we see milk spilt on the floor it remains a mystery until we look at the evidence: the paw prints of a cat might suggest answers to us. Reading signs has a grammar and syntax that we already possess as human beings. While an understanding of the classical, Christian and cultural symbols depicted in the tarot can help us to gain the historical nuance of the cards, we still use our common sense to read, within the context of the question that triggered the laying of cards.

There are no esoteric methods of reading given in this book because, in telling the story of untold tarot, it is the cards that must speak for themselves, without having to carry a load of extra esoteric data. The cards that we read require us to join up the signs into statements and understandings that answer real questions. We don't need to read them with the help of the zodiac or the Tree of Life: this is surely like reading a French novel with the help of a Russian dictionary. Some people may see the jettisoning of esoteric methods of reading as a betrayal of "original methods" and spurn common-sense reading methods as being "too literal." But the ability to read the signs around us is a skill that we apply pragmatically. When someone comes for a reading, they don't want to know about the movements of planets or where on the Tree of Life they are currently located, but rather about how their holiday plans are going to work out, or how the intransigence of their partner is going to impact on the family. Ultimately, it is the cards themselves that tell us how to read them.

READING CARTOMANTICALLY

Cartomancy, or the reading of playing cards for divination, developed massively in the late 18th century, when methods of reading from playing cards gained vast popularity. This was largely because Etteilla, the father of modern carto-mancy, wrote the first "how-to" book on card divination in 1770, using a piquet deck of thirty-two playing cards that he modestly called "*le Petit Etteilla.*" In his second edition of *La Seule Manière de Tirer Les Cartes* of 1773, he reports that he learned this divinatory skill from "an old Piedmontese, called Alexis, whom he met at Lamballe in Brittany." [23] Piedmont is the region of Italy that immediately borders France and, as we have seen, is the area from whence the tarot traveled from Italy into France, only to return to Italy a couple of centuries later, in the form of the *Tarot de Marseille* pattern. Italian and French methods of cartomancy show many regional variations, and most probably stem from playing cards rather than tarot. However, since the trumps of the tarot have a separate derivation from the pips and courts, which derive from playing cards, this works to our advantage. Even today in Italy, the playing card suits are still the tarot suits, complete with the figure of the Knight, not the French suits with Hearts, Spades, Clubs and Diamonds. What Etteilla began, others have gone on to develop, with playing card cartomancy establishing its own distinct forms in different European countries.

Those unfamiliar with historical tarots may feel that there should be some kind of fixed choreography, but this is not the case. In this book, I show two methods of reading pips: in the first, the reader can make associations between the suits and numbers of the pips to create a myriad of variations, while in the second, I have given a set of cartomantic meanings which are different from modern 20th-century tarots, for those who like a system they can learn. With the latter method, the guiding principles are also based upon the major themes of the trumps. You are at liberty to use whichever you prefer or to find your own meanings. My own background lies in tarot, small oracle and playing card cartomancy methods, and I move fluidly between these methods.

When you read in this cartomantic way, when there are no pictures, things change; you may not always receive an instant impression when you have a set of pips, but have to rely upon other skills. This learning can arise from the remembering and weaving together of number and suit qualities, for example, but reading cartomantically involves both visual impression and verbal skills. As with the reading of pictorial cards, you make choices as you read, relating them to the question – except that, now, it is the cards that are talking. The positioning and directionality of the cards may also suggest parts of the story, and we shall explore that in more detail in Chapter 6.

One of the other results of reading cartomantically is that readings come out quickly and concisely: this brevity shocks some taromancers, who feel that their more leisurely expository method is somehow disrespected. But being concise is good if it speaks to the question – further cards can be chosen, if more detail is needed. Most of the reading formats in this book are short, but some use many more cards than are normally read, which initially may look alarming. However, when you read concisely, so many cards are not such a challenge, because you home in on – for example in a tableau – the position of the significator and which cards surround it. Sometimes it is a matter of locating the querent within the landscape of their lives, so that you are able to give the best advice.

Another adjustment you might have to make in historical reading methods is that pre-set spreads, whereby each position has its own meaning, are rarer than linear or tableaux-style formats. I have given many pre-set spreads for the learner to gain some handholds, but the predominant, older method of reading is in lines and ranks, and in associating the cards in a variety of ways.

Some of the methods in this book require cards to be read in a secondary layer, by pairing or mirroring cards. This is a cartomantic method that often reveals a clear dynamic, so if anything hasn't been precise enough on the first reading of the cards, information can be discerned more clearly or confirmed from the next layer down – often in stark or obvious relief. However, reading the secondary layer isn't always necessary if the story is clear.

Those who prefer some kind of fixed choreography for reading historical tarots can rely on the two methods I've given, but these are not the only way. Alongside these two methods, you will also retain the use of your eyes to read and so find a completely fresh way of reading that never has the same meaning twice. By looking at the visual sense of a line, you can gain immediate revelation and a sense of what the cards are showing you, and this primary method is how you will initially assess the cards. This style of reading is still cartomantic but, like the tarocchino method, is brief and factual: it does not require any pre-learned meaning.

Opposite is a short line of cards laid for a younger man who's seeking work after an absence from his country. He asks, "What do I need to focus upon to make this transition and earn an income?" Cover the paragraphs below the image and see what sense you gain from just looking at these cards; ignore the King of Batons to begin with.

Reading from left to right, we see a cautious young man defensively drawing his sword, looking over his right shoulder. Behind him are two coins. A woman opens the lion's mouth and looks at people emerging from their graves, called by the angel's trumpet. Taking the question into this quick visual impression, we could say, "Time to shake off the last venue and prepare to accept the new offer, with some retraining, so that you can make a comeback to the workplace." This way of reading is making a story that connects each card into one telling, like beads threaded on a string, but it is based entirely on the visual clues.

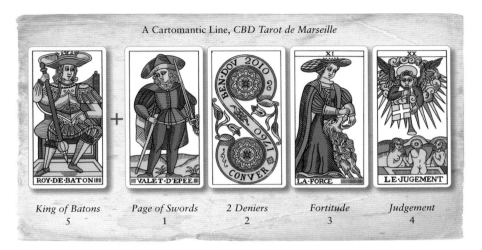

A Cartomantic Line, *CBD Tarot de Marseille*

King of Batons	Page of Swords	2 Deniers	Fortitude	Judgement
5	1	2	3	4

Here's how we reached this conclusion: since a man is asking the question, we can assign the Page of Swords to him as the significator, or card that represents him (see Chapter 6), and read what it tells us about him. His defensive posture and the way in which he looks backwards suggests that he is still dealing with some older issue from his last overseas post. 2 Deniers could be the income he is asking about, literally representing coins, and a new offer of work. But Fortitude is looking away from them, turning towards Judgement, which represents his comeback to the workplace, so there is something he needs to attend to first. I also want to see what the Page of Swords is looking back at, and ask the man to draw a new card, placing it in front of the line. Now the Page of Swords is looking at the King of Batons, who represents the old boss with whom he's had an unfortunate and aggravating entanglement: the two courts face up to each other, so it still rankles. Fortitude is suggesting that he bridge this gap by taking the new offer as shown in 2 Deniers, and learn how to use his skills in a different way, maybe by retraining, as we have Judgement as the last card – a comeback in a new way.

In this short line, we have used the skills of initial visual impression, the juxtapositioning of cards in relationship and their directional aspect which follows the gaze of the characters on the cards, to find the story. We will build on these skills further in Chapters 5 and 6, after we have looked at the trumps, pips and courts in Chapters 2, 3 and 4. So get out your cards and prepare to meet the eloquent trumps.

CHAPTER 2

THE ELOQUENT TRUMPS

Tarot is what my heart's become:
A Fool through the world, on fate's spar,
Whirling with Angel, Sun, Moon, Star.
Wandering to escape the Burning House,
Despising the Devil, calling on Death,
As a Hanging One with his last breath.
The Hunchback shines his light up to the Wheel,
By Force conducted to the hands of Love,
Triumphal Car victoriously above.
Temperance, Popes and Juggler,
Continually jostle about my heart:
Your love plays Tarot's game in every part.

ANONYMOUS 16TH-CENTURY ITALIAN VILLANELLE, *Taroch è Diventato il Mio Core*,
translated by Caitlín Matthews

THE ICONOGRAPHY OF THE TRIUMPHS

The twenty-two cards that make a tarot different from a deck of playing cards are called the trumps, which take their name from the word "triumph." The military triumphal processions of ancient Rome that celebrated returning commanders were ways of revealing the extent of the Roman army's conquest, as well as of honoring its troops. Similar processions through the streets of Europe were part of medieval Catholic life: representations and tableaux of religious subjects, and the legends of saints, were drawn on carts and shown at festival time. The royal entry of monarchs and rulers into a city was marked by similar festivities. Carnival processions and more literary pageants based upon classical triumphal processions were enacted, all to impress the populace, or to act as propaganda.

Tarot cards came into being in the early 15th century in Northern Italy. They were first called *carte di trionfi* or "triumph cards," since they followed a sequence like the unfolding of a triumphal pageant that people witnessed in the street, but their subjects were also known from literary works like Petrarch's *Trionfi* and Dante's *Divina Comedia*. This has given us the word "trump," meaning "a trick taken in a game of cards," whereby one suit "trumps" or beats another one.

We do not know the exact processes by which the suits of the trumps came into being, but they depict allegorical figures that were standardized from very early onwards. While many attempts have been made to understand the sequence and origins of the trumps, it is clear that all twenty-two cards derive from a variety of different sources:

Biblical or Christian The Tower, from the Tower of Babel in Genesis 11:1–9; Judgement, from the Last Judgement; the World, from the depiction of Christ in glory with the Four Evangelists; and the Devil.

Celestial Bodies Sun, Moon, Star.

Cardinal Virtues Fortitude, Justice and Temperance all derive their symbology via Plato's definition of the virtues, through Western iconography. Fortitude acquires the column broken by Samson, before it changes into a woman wrestling a lion; Justice has the sword and balances of the Greek goddess Themis. (See page 142 for more on the Virtues.)

Classical Tradition Wheel of Fortune, from late antiquity; the Hermit, which derives from depictions of time, from the Greek god Cronos; the Lovers with Eros, from the Greek and Roman versions of the god of love, Eros and Cupid respectively; and the Chariot, from Roman triumphal and medieval processions.

The Estate of Man Seven figures are derived from the human condition: Fool, Juggler, Hanged Man and the two pairs of imperial and papal figures, Emperor and Empress, Popess and Pope.

Death Each of these seven is subject to Death, who is the gatherer of all that is mortal.

We see how the tarot derives from a synthesis of different cultural and religious traditions through time, woven together to create a world view that speaks to all conditions about many topics. Every generation views the tarot through its own cultural filter, a feature we will pursue further in Chapter 7.

THE ORDER OF THE TRUMPS

While trump images have retained a standard depiction, with some variation, the numeration of the trumps has not always been consistent. Ferrara and Bolognese patterns are slightly different from the *Tarot de Marseille* pattern that is now considered to be the standardized numeration. Throughout this book, I have used *Tarot de Marseille* numeration, except in the *Ferrarese* and *Bolognese* decks. The Ferrara school of tarot has a different sequence, and this is still echoed in some modern Italian decks.

The modern numeration and switched positions of VIII Justice with XI Strength, which now appear in most post 20th-century tarots, follows a decision made by the Hermetic Order of the Golden Dawn to make every kabbalistic and planetary correspondence accord with the trumps. This has muddied the waters rather. The Golden Dawn made Justice correspond to Libra, and Fortitude to Leo, in accordance with the emblems appearing on the cards, thus making them appear in positions XI and VIII respectively. The *Tarot de Marseille* and older decks weren't interested in planetary ascription, and so Justice and Fortitude in this book return to their usual places, at VIII and XI respectively.

According to Michael Dummet, three categories of tarot order exist: type A is based around the Italian city states of Bologna, Ferrara and Florence; type B is based around Venice and Ferrara; and type C is based around Milan, which is now the standard order for most Western tarots. In this sequence, the Fool is not shown, since he is not numbered.[24]

As we can see, the most unusual order is found in the Ferrarese tarots, and the most customary to our eyes is the Milanese tarot order, from which Northern Italian tradition the *Tarot de Marseille* derives. The Bolognese-style order keeps all the Cardinal Virtues together, and has the Angel (Judgement) as the last card. The Ferrara-style order pairs the two imperial and papal figures together, and brings Temperance up before Love in a pairing that speaks of chastity and erotic love, as well as moving Justice up between Angel and the World. There are many other regional Italian differences, especially in the Sicilian tradition.

The villanelle at the head of this chapter enumerates the Bolognese order of the trumps, in descending order, as is usual. We can guess it is from pre 18th-century Bologna because it speaks of "the Popes," which was how the two papal cards and the imperial couple together were known. This derives from the way they were played in *Tarocchino Bolognese*, which reduces the tarot pack from seventy-eight to sixty-two cards, by leaving out the pips numbered 2–5. The poem also mentions the Hunchback, or *Il Gobbo*, which is the local name for the Hermit, while "the Burning House" is what is normally depicted on the Tower card in this tradition.

A: BOLOGNA/FLORENCE	B: FERRARA/VENICE	C: MILAN
Juggler	Juggler	Juggler
Popess	Empress	Popess
Empress	Emperor	Empress
Emperor	Popess	Emperor
Pope	Pope	Pope
Love	Temperance	Love
Chariot	Love	Chariot
Temperance	Chariot	
Justice		Justice
Fortitude	Fortitude	Hermit
Wheel	Wheel	Wheel
Hermit	Hermit	Fortitude
Hanged Man	Hanged Man	Hanged Man
Death	Death	Death
		Temperance
Devil	Devil	Devil
Tower	Tower	Tower
Star	Star	Star
Moon	Moon	Moon
Sun	Sun	Sun
World	Angel	Angel
	Justice	
Angel	World	World

The varying orders of early Italian trumps

THE SPEAKING TRUMPS

In the following pages, the descriptions and the direction in which each character is facing are taken from the *Tarot de Marseille*: the latter pertains to the viewer's line of sight, so the Empress is looking to her own left, which corresponds to the reader's right. This directionality changes in different tarots, especially in those *Tarots de Marseille* where the woodblock has been printed backwards: please work with what your own cards are revealing. The trumps are illustrated from a selection of the tarots used in this book, which may vary from the *Tarot de Marseille* descriptions given. In that tarot, there are only five cards that look straight ahead at the viewer: Hanged Man, Justice, Devil, Sun and Judgement. I have suggested ways in which you might determine what they might reveal in a reading.

Remember, too, that the symbol of the upright arrow ↑ shows the customary or uncomplicated sides of each trump, while the downward arrow ↓ shows its ambivalent, unhelpful or blocked aspects (see page 154). In older styles of reading, tarot cards are kept upright, although a card may show less helpful aspects when we read it. Beneath each entry are keywords that help you to stay on track, plus brief examples of combinations: these, too, will become mutable as you read them.

THE TRUMPS

0 Fool
(page 44)

I Juggler
(page 46)

II Popess
(page 48)

III Empress
(page 50)

IV Emperor
(page 52)

V Pope
(page 54)

VI Lovers
(page 56)

VII Chariot
(page 58)

VIII Justice
(page 60)

IX Hermit
(page 62)

X Wheel of
Fortune
(page 64)

XI Fortitude
(page 66)

XII Hanged
Man
(page 68)

XIII Death
(page 70)

XIV
Temperance
(page 72)

XV Devil
(page 74)

XVI Tower
(page 76)

XVII Star
(page 78)

XVIII Moon
(page 80)

XIX Sun
(page 82)

XX Judgement
(page 84)

XXI World
(page 86)

Tarot de Marseille Pierre Madenié 1709

— 0 FOOL —

I never saw fool yet that thought himself other than wise.

SIR THOMAS MORE,
A Dialogue of Comfort Against Tribulation

French: *Le Mat*
Italian: *Il Matto*
English: *The Fool*
Direction: *To the right*

KEYWORDS

↑ Innocence, carefree, optimism, spontaneity, foolishness. Unburdened, uncommitted, wandering, acting the fool. Unpredictability. Humor.
↓ Naivety, foolishness, recklessness, risk-taking, irresponsible, disorganization, craziness, heedless action. A Walter Mitty-style enthusiasm. Sloth.

AS A PERSON

Vagabond, hitch-hiker, wayfarer, pilgrim, vagrant, mad person. An unreliable person. Someone who disgraces you.

EXAMPLES

- Fool + 3 Batons: the innocent rushes towards a lucky opening.
- Fortitude + Fool + Hanged Man: a lack of self-discipline is leading you to risk being pilloried.

The Fool walks along a bumpy road, attired in cap and bells over his stripy tunic. He has his eyes set on the horizon and so doesn't yet see the cat or dog that is about to scratch him through a gap in his hose. He has two sticks: with one he strides out along the road, while the other is slung over his right shoulder carrying his belongings in a cloth.

The Fool has his own title, but no number in the tarot. He is out of sequence, and usually appears last in any older listings, if he appears at all. *Il Matto* means "the crazy or mad one," with the French name deriving from this Italian meaning. The Fool was called "the excuse" when playing trick-taking games, since one might use him as a means of playing a card when unable "to follow suit." This sense of his substitution for another card has had a further modern development: since the mid 20th century it has been a popular understanding in tarot circles for the Fool to be seen as a kind of everyman, and his lack of position as a means of seeing the sequence of trumps as "the Fool's Journey," or an unfolding development that he undergoes – a concept popularized by taromancer Eden Gray from 1970.[25] This spotlight on the Fool is radically contrary to his role in historical reading. (Note that the modern Joker from playing cards may have resonance with the Fool in people's minds, but that the Joker did not appear until the late 19th century, first arriving in America.) The 16th-century *Leber Tarot* of Rouen, of which only thirty cards remain, shows the Fool as a warrior going headlong into battle, with the Latin tag of *Velim Fundam Dari Mihi,* or "I wish the purse to be given me" – a reference to the payment of a mercenary.[26] Francesca Piscina, writing in 1565, says of the Fool that "he looks behind towards a mirror," showing up what is hidden.[27]

When the Fool comes into a reading you can expect some unpredictability. As well as the kind of court Fool, licensed to speak the truth via his merry japes, he can reveal a foolish optimism or even heedless action. If he has an agenda, it will only have a mayfly's attention span, for he has no staying power; mostly, to what others feel is serious, he shows indifference or else makes fun of them. Whether he comes with cap and bells or is just a vagrant, the Fool shows you what you are not taking seriously, which will be the card he faces. Very occasionally, you get the sense that you are being laughed at.

*Facsimile Italian Renaissance
Woodcut Tarocchi*

— I JUGGLER —

*He who seeks to deceive will always
find someone who will allow
himself to be deceived.*

NICCOLÒ MACHIAVELLI, *The Prince*

French: *Le Bateleur*
Italian: *Il Bagattello or Il Bagatto*
English and Esoteric: *Magician*
Direction: *Left*

KEYWORDS

↑ Crafty and dexterous, ingenuity. Having initiative, self-confidence,
chutzpah. Performing, persuading, spinning a tale. Being streetwise,
calculating.
↓ Using sleight of hand, cheating, deception, trickery. Manipulation,
poor planning, latent talents, dishonest trading. Being distracted.

AS A PERSON

Showman, performer, entrepreneur, charlatan, a mountebank,
street-seller, fence, cheat, scam-artist, a charmer or fast-talker,
a flâneur.

EXAMPLES

• 7 Swords + Juggler: seizing the chance to make a presentation.
• 7 Cups + Juggler + King of Swords: an offer you can't refuse, you
are persuading yourself, but it becomes a hard taskmaster.

The Juggler stands before a table which bears the implements of his trade: the balls and cups, the coins, knife and bag out of which he conjures things to amaze us. On his head is a wide-brimmed hat as he stands confidently, a baton raised to complete his showman's trick.

The Bateleur/Bagattello has the meaning of "street performer," someone who does a show or demonstrates tricks in a street context. It was Court de Gébelin, and most especially Eliphas Lévi, who were responsible for changing his name from Juggler to Magician, elevating his status from street entertainer to that of hermetic magician – something that is not borne out in pre-esoteric tradition.[28] In fact, the tarot card most closely associated with magicians is the Star which, in Bolognese tradition, depicts the Three Magi. It is for this reason that I've chosen to call him the "Juggler" here, for the only kind of magic he deals in is conjuring tricks. The Juggler represents the kind of street salesman who sets up his stall at a moment's notice to sell off some shoddy, knocked-down goods, or the kind of showman who plays "hunt the lady" with his three-card trick, inveigling you into speculation. Interestingly, the Juggler has on his table representatives of the four suits: coins, cups and two blades, while in his hand is a baton.

The Juggler observes society closely and there is little that he doesn't take note of, but his art is that of distraction. If he comes into a reading when your question concerns someone's performance or guile, you can place a card beneath him to see what is hiding under his table, unseen. The card to the left of the Juggler is what you are expected to see, while the card to the right may show what you are being distracted away from.

❧

— II POPESS —

LA·PAPESSE

CBD Tarot de Marseille

*What is better than wisdom?
Woman.
And what is better than a good woman?
Nothing.*

GEOFFREY CHAUCER, *The Tale of Melibeus*

French: *La Papesse*
Italian: *La Papesse*
English: *The Popess*
Esoteric: *The High Priestess*
Direction: *Left*

KEYWORDS

↑ Knowledge. Mystery, wisdom, revelation, spiritual counsel. Learning, guidance, teaching, study. Sub rosa, silence, discretion, secrets, meditation. Female suffrage and liberation. Inviolability.
↓ Hidden agendas, needing to listen to the inner voice, rumor, false revelations, spiritual credulity, tampered with.

AS A PERSON

A woman of spiritual authority, an abbess, fortune-teller, oracle, diviner, sibyl. Midwife, godmother, aunt, confidante. Headmistress, teacher, a single woman. A transgendered or cross-dressing man.

EXAMPLES

- Popess + Moon: a seer or clairvoyant.
- 5 Swords + Popess + Temperance: your beliefs can guide you, giving you access to the voice of your conscience.

A grave lady under the canopy of a cloth of estate sits with an open book upon her lap. She is crowned with the triple tiara of the papacy. She is so opulently draped that we cannot see what manner of form she has, though her face is beardless. Her book is open for all to see, but her wisdom has to be discovered by those who learn of her.

The legend behind this card is the semi-apocryphal story about Pope Joan, found first in *Liber Pontificalis* by the archivist Anastasius Bibliothecarius (d. 886); it became very popular in the 13th century, spawning many re-tellings and artworks. Joan, known in her male guise as John Anglicus (English John), grew up being able to read and write; she took refuge in a German monastery as a monk and worked her way up to becoming Pope. All went well until she started to give birth, the fruit of a dalliance with her lover, during a papal procession; as the truth was startlingly revealed, Joan was torn to pieces by the hysterical Roman mob. Historical opinion is divided, citing her possible existence during the 11th century when there were many anti-popes. Others have posited that the Popess's origins lie in Sister Manfreda, a nun of the Umiliata order of the heretical Gugliemites, who followed the ideology popularized by the 13th-century Franciscan visionary St Joachim of Fiore.[29] Manfreda was a member of the Visconti family and it is believed by some that the Popess card in that tarot depicts her. Both Joan and Manfreda, like the Alexandrian Greek mathematician Hypatia, were women brought down by their learning.

The Popess makes a pair with the Pope, as one of the two rulers governing the spiritual domain, just as the Empress and Emperor govern the terrestrial realm. Her learning and wisdom set her mythically within the archetype of Sophia or Wisdom, and what is hidden or not yet revealed. In some decks, such as the 16th-century *Tarot de Paris*, the Popess carries a key, showing that she governs discretion and secrets. In a reading, the Popess is often showing you a wisdom you hadn't been considering, or urging you to discretion, so see which card she is looking at.

Tarot de Marseille Pierre Madenié 1709

— III EMPRESS —

The proper duty of the wise queen and princess is to be the means of peace and concord, to work for the avoidance of war.

CHRISTINE DE PISAN, *The Treasure of the City of Ladies*

French: *L'Imperatrice*
Italian: *L'Imperatrice*
English: *The Empress*
Direction: *Right*

KEYWORDS

↑ Beauty, abundance. Fertility, motherhood. Harmony, grace. Beneficence, care, protection. Sponsorship, creation, culture. Design, ornament, luxury. Peace. Nurture. The natural world. Feminism and women's mysteries.
↓ Creative block, dependence on others, over-protective, poor design, unaesthetic. An unwanted pregnancy, infertility.

AS A PERSON

Mother, goddess, cult-woman, female celebrity, a pregnant woman, a manager. A madam.

EXAMPLES

- King of Cups + Empress: the artistic man presents the natural world in his art.
- 4 Cups + Empress + 2 Swords: your marriage bed needs protection or you will be separating from each other.

On a throne, whose back suggests heart-shaped wings, sits a regal woman. Encircled by her protective right arm and resting on her hip is a shield upon which is depicted the imperial eagle; we never doubt that everything and everyone in her imperial domain is loved. In her left hand is a sceptre, topped with the sphere and surmounted by the Christian cross. Her overtunic covers an enveloping blue dress, and her capacious lap is wide.

The role of the Empress is to share the sovereignty of the Emperor, and she makes a pair with him as temporal or exoteric rulers: under their domain is the whole of the realm. In the *Leber Tarot* of Rouen, the Empress card has the Latin tag of *Omnium Dominatrix*, or "mistress of all."[30] In classical history, the empresses of Rome were known as *augusta* and few, other than Livia, wife of Augustus, played an important or notable part in ruling but, in Byzantium, such women as Theodora and Irene of Athens became regnant empresses. By the early Middle Ages, the Holy Roman Emperors were created by the Pope, enabling them to play a much larger role in European life, being elected theoretically as "the first among equals" among Christian monarchs. The eagle upon the shield of both Empress and Emperor is the *reichsadler* or Imperial Eagle. It is a single- rather than a double-bodied eagle, so we can tell that it derives from the mid 14th century and not later, as this shield was borne by the Holy Roman Emperors from the House of Luxembourg at that time; afterwards, the double eagle replaced the single one.

The Empress holds all things peacefully and gracefully, but with authority. She oversees the whole realm, sponsoring its culture and achievements, building up its character and ensuring that things are made beautifully. In a reading, the Empress prompts you to look at what is going to make your life more beautiful and harmonious, or shows you what it is that needs your special protection or attention, so see which card is to the right of her.

Tarot de Marseille Pierre Madenié 1709

— IV EMPEROR —

*There is nothing that wins over the
hearts of a ruler's subjects more,
nor that draws them to their lord
so much, as when they find gentleness
and kindness in him.*

CHRISTINE DE PISAN, *The Treasure of the City of Ladies*

French: *Le Empereur*
Italian: *L'Imperatore*
English: *The Emperor*
Direction: *Left*

KEYWORDS

↑ Authority. Organization. Protection, stability. Fatherhood, potency.
Politics. Dynamism. Authorized things. The Masculine and men's
mysteries.
↓ Domination, excessive control, rigidity, inflexibility, tyranny, abuse
of power. Authoritarianism. Militancy, belligerence.

AS A PERSON

Father, a ruler, a leader, commander, a dictator, autocrat, governor,
patron, boss, a Mafia "Godfather."

EXAMPLES

- Emperor + 2 Batons: a business meeting with the boss.
- Knight of Cups + Emperor + Page of Cups: ambitious to be a man,
  your son is impressionable and needs your guidance.

*A man with a crown over his helmet leans against a throne, with his left
leg braced and his right leg crossed over it. He confidently holds out
his sceptre with its cruciform cross upon its orb. He means business, for
his left hand clutches his belt. Around his neck is a heavy gold chain
with a circular pendant, and at his feet is a shield upon which is
spread the imperial eagle.*

The role of emperor was reinvented in the 9th century when Charlemagne
was elected the first Holy Roman Emperor, a papal appointment whereby
he might be the protector of Christendom in Europe. With the Empress, the
Emperor makes up the imperial pair who rule over a larger domain than just
a single country: they have in their care the very roots of civilization. Although
the papal pair oversee its spiritual guardianship, the imperial pair protect,
defend, uphold and build up that civilization. In the later Middle Ages the
imperium became confined to the Germanic territories. The imperial eagle on
the Emperor's shield symbolizes the highest possible protection, as the eagle
flies highest over its domain.

Many modern readings see the Emperor as simply a patriarchal man, especially during the rise of 20th-century feminism. While the Emperor can indeed
show off his machismo, he is ultimately a civilized ruler and the well-being of
his realm on all levels is important. The main reason that many rulers learned
warcraft was to protect and defend their boundaries; when it came to expanding their realm by waging war upon an opponent or putting down rebellion,
they were equally ferocious in attack.

In a reading, the Emperor will show what he is promoting in the card facing
him. Behind him there may be matters that need his authoritative care.

— V POPE —

CBD Tarot de Marseille

> *The greatness of contemplation can be given to none but those who love.*

POPE ST GREGORY THE GREAT, *Homilies on Ezekiel*

French: *Le Pape*
Italian: *Il Pape*
English: *The Pope*
Esoteric: *The Hierophant*
Direction: *Right*

KEYWORDS

↑ Tradition, heritage. Religion. Revelation, inspiration, insight. Spiritual counsel. Education, tuition. Mandated, ordained, blessed. Mediation. Marriage ceremony.

↓ Restriction, challenging the status quo, unconventionality, cults, spiritual corruption or subversion. Divorce.

AS A PERSON

Godfather, celebrant, priest, cult-man, tutor, headmaster.

EXAMPLES

- Pope + World: a worldwide religious movement.
- Devil + Pope + Queen of Swords: a deeply subversive holy man fancies the divorcée; what she thinks is a blessing may be a trap.

A bearded pope sits upon a two-pillared chair. Upon his head is the triple tiara, giving spiritual authority as he raises his gloved right hand in blessing. In his left, he holds a triple patriarchal cross. He is attired in ample vestments, trimmed with gold. At his feet kneel in homage two tonsured clerics, one of whom stretches out his hand.

With the Popess, the Pope makes up the pair of spiritual rulers. The voice of spirit is mediated through them. In the *Leber Tarot* of Rouen, the Latin tag on the Pope card is *Pontifex Pontificium*, or "the high priest of high priests," from the Latin title of a priest as a "bridge" or mediator.[31] The papal title derives from the ancient Roman title for the pagan Pontifex Maximus, and is now accorded to the Pope in the Vatican, who is still elected by the College of Cardinals. The figure of the Pope became invested with mystique and notoriety alike over the years, especially with the coming of the Protestant Reformation, which created a significant break with the power of the Catholic Church that he represented. Instead of a figure of power, the Pope became, for Protestants, the epitome of spiritual corruption, leading to anti-papal protests. By the 18th century, revolutionary views had spread through Europe, further devaluing views of the papacy.

The placement of the Pope before the Lovers is interesting; one of the traditional meanings for him has been matrimony, since he appears to bless the Lovers. Both images were taken into the *Grand Etteilla Tarot* by Etteilla as card 13, which shows the Pope blessing a couple. The triumph of Chastity over Love is one of Petrarch's images in his *Trionfi,* where Chastity holding a palm leaf is led on a car with a bevy of virgins accompanying her.[32]

In a reading, the Pope blesses or confirms the card to the right: if the facing card reveals a dubious message, he may be showing his ambivalence, and you may need to revert to the blocked or difficult meaning to show what is being said.

— VI LOVERS —

Playing Marseille

That conqueror, moving first to the attack, Held in his hands an arrow and a bow, The bowstring drawn already to his ear.

PETRARCH, *The Triumph of Chastity*

French: *L'Amoreux*
Italian: *Gli Amante*
English: *The Lovers*
Direction: *Eros looks right; the male lover, left; the older woman, right; the young woman, left.*
Decide whose is the strongest gaze!

KEYWORDS

↑ Sexual love, emotional ties, relating. Desire, passion. Choice, decision. Reassurance in your relationship. First love. The voice of the heart.
↓ Disharmonious relations, unbalanced desires, vacillation, a choice between heart or head, a love triangle, ambivalence.

AS A PERSON

A couple, someone on the pull, a marriage-arranger.

EXAMPLES

- Lovers + 6 Cups: a past lover for whom you still hold a candle.
- Fool + Lovers + King of Batons: you feel you should love the blow-in because he is so cute, but what you really want is a mature and dynamic lover.

A young man stands between an older woman and a younger one.
What is the relationship between them? It really isn't clear, but
from the man's stance, with one foot going in either direction, some
choice is involved. The matron puts her left hand upon his shoulder,
while the young woman lays her left hand upon his chest.
Above all three flies Eros or Cupid, appearing from a window into
heaven, with his bow ready bent: it is aimed at the man's heart.

In Greek myth, even Zeus was afraid of Eros, so devastating is the effect of love, whose desire and passion alights like a raptor upon the unsuspecting individual, changing every aspect of his or her outlook. Eros or Cupid appears in the first of Petrarch's *Trionfi*, riding high over the procession.[33] The French title of the card is singular, "the Lover," while Italian and English versions put the title in the plural. There are two kinds of *Tarot de Marseille*: in the class I, Eros is blindfolded – denoting love being blind – while in the class II variation, Eros's eyes are unbound. In the *Tarot de Marseille*, both the man and the young woman are looking left – the man looks at the matron, while the young woman looks at the man. In such an array, it appears that the matron is the man's mother, who is commending him to his partner as the younger woman declares her love for him. It is a three-way look, because the matron looks at the younger woman.

Certainly, the matron has a headdress of what looks to be laurel leaves – the tree of chastity – while the young woman wears a headdress full of fertile seeds or tightly closed buds; this seems like a reference to Apollo and Daphne. Apollo desired Daphne, but she did not reciprocate his love. In her attempt to flee his embraces, she begged to be turned into a form that would thwart Apollo, finally becoming a laurel tree. From this tree, Apollo took the leaves as a sign that he would always hold her love sacred. The laurel thus becomes a sign of undying virtue and chastity, now being assigned to victors, and to honor artists and musicians whose art comes under the aegis of Apollo.

In a reading, the Lovers can be speaking about a relationship or where your desires are disposed, as well as the nature of a decision. If it is the latter, then look at the cards on either side: the thing you *should do* is on the left and the thing you *want to do* is on the right. Place a random card over it, to signify where Eros is guiding you.

— VII CHARIOT —

LE CHARIOT

CBD Tarot de Marseille

Folk armed alike with valor
and with steel,
As in the triumphs that in olden times
Proceeded through the sacred
ways of Rome.

PETRARCH, *The Triumph of Fame*

French: *Le Chariot*
Italian: *Il Carro*
English: *The Chariot*
Direction: *Left*

KEYWORDS

↑ Triumph, victory, reward, prestige, honor, celebrity, fame.
Self-discipline, clear intentions. Travel, progress. Will, control,
determination, insight.
↓ Lack of control and direction, waywardly out of kilter, over-confident,
dragging away the spoils, notoriety, boasting of your win.

AS A PERSON

A traveler, driver, the winner, a celebrity, prize-giver, a general.

EXAMPLES

- Chariot + Moon: traveling through unknown regions.
- 9 Swords + Chariot + Death: you want to go it alone and bring home
the rewards, but it's going to take the last thing you have.

Under a curtained awning, a charioteer rides in a chariot borne by two horses. He wears a crown upon his head, and in his right hand is a sceptre. The charioteer is attired in armour, with lunar faces as epaulettes upon either shoulder. Before him, two horses run: although they are harnessed, they are controlled without any reins, even though the terrain over which they ride is rough and uneven. Direction is maintained and the wheels turn around through will and attention alone.

From the Sanscrit *Rigveda* to the Irish *Audacht Morainn*, the charioteer is cited as the one who keeps things straight. His progress in the chariot is likened to that of a ruler who maintains the kingdom on a good course, without deviation or shaking the whole edifice of government to pieces. In Plato's *Phaedrus*, the chariot's two horses are described thus: the horse on the right is the nobler one, for he is a "lover of honor with modesty and self-control."[34] The horse on the left is uglier and wilder, for he is "companion to wild boasts and indecency." Did the creator of the Chariot card have Plato in mind? On this card, the horses appear to be pulling in opposite directions.

In the *Tarot de Marseille* sequence, the Chariot precedes Justice, which is what the good ruler must provide for the good of all: fairness, truth, good government. In history and myth, the triumphal chariot is that of Mars, the reward of a general who returns successfully from the wars as the conquering hero and processes with the spoils from his sacking of foreign cities: he is acclaimed by his peers and returns in triumph as the crowned victor. The *Trionfi* of Petrarch depict Fame as the fourth chariot, borne by elephants, which overcomes Death itself. In the *Leber Tarot*, the Latin tag for the Chariot is *Victoriae Premium*, or "the reward of victory."[35]

In a reading where the Chariot appears, check the steering of the issue: unlike the lover in the last card, who might be choosing between two different ways, the charioteer may look to left or right, but he has to steer straight. Where he looks, the card to the left reveals what he wants to roll out.

— VIII JUSTICE —

Vandenborre Tarot

*Justice is the constant and perpetual
wish to render everyone his due.*

EMPEROR JUSTINIAN, *The Institutes of Justinian*

French: *La Justice*
Italian: *La Giudizia*
English: *Justice*
Esoteric: *Appears at position XI*
Direction: *Faces forward*

KEYWORDS

↑ Equity, impartiality, fairness. Perception of motives, scrutiny.
Integrity, honesty, truth. Being heard. A court case, law or process.
An investigation or examination. Sharing out equally, being even-
handed. Human rights, codes of honor. Precision. Mitigation.
Vindication. Being authentic.

↓ Unfairness, inequality, lack of accountability, dishonesty, injustice.
Inability to judge clearly, criticism. Not being listened to. Prejudice and
partiality. Corrupt laws. Blame. Punishment. A sense of persecution.

AS A PERSON

A judge, assessor, examiner, inspector, member of the police, lawyer.

EXAMPLES

- Justice + 5 Cups: negotiating the household rules.
- Ace of Cups + Justice + Page of Batons: the upheaval at home is caused
  by restraining a petulant youth.

With equitable poise, Justice sits upon her throne. In her left hand is a naked sword and in her right hand a pair of scales. She faces directly out, to signify that she is fair to all who come before her: punishment and mercy both lie within her gift. She sits upon uneven ground, yet she is crowned and wears a necklace of golden links. No matter what the terrain, her eyes see into every case.

J ustice is one of the Cardinal Virtues, along with Temperance, Fortitude and Prudence. She always appears as female, with the two-edged sword of equity that can cut both ways – to deal punishment or to defend the innocent – and the scales which weigh the truth or lack of it in her balances. Mythically, Justice is resonant with the Greek Themis and the Egyptian Ma'at, those who bring harmony to the world: the reverse of *ma'at* or good order was *isfet* or disorder and violence.

Despite her very neutrality and fairness, Justice is rarely clean-cut in our world: some will always feel hard done by her, as guilt or innocence are not so easily discerned. The justice that orders our world is innately seen in codes of law and government worldwide, from the laws of the Babylonian king Hammurabi, promulgated in about 1792 BC, to the Universal Declaration of Human Rights in 1948. In our own time, human rights still do not obtain in every part of the world, and many basic rights are still absent, so that Justice is needed as never before.

In a reading, Justice is uncompromising and unswerving in her regard, as one of the five cards that look straight at the viewer: you know that the truth is expected of you. (See page 179.) The cards on either side of her can show the truth or lies that are being sifted. An innate sense of guilt or innocence is often covered up by the human need to be right, and so it is easy to fall into blaming others for wrongdoing, proclaiming oneself to be the innocent party. Be careful not to confuse Justice with the Queen of Swords.

⚜

Vergnano Tarot

— IX HERMIT —

Considering now the brevity of life,
And striving to make ready for the end:
This morn I was a child,
and now am old.

PETRARCH, *The Triumph of Time*

French: *L'Hermite*
Italian: *L'Erimita, Il Gobbo*
English: *The Hermit*
Direction: *Left*

KEYWORDS

↑ Guidance. Introspection. Maturity, old. Memory, foresight. Time. Listening to the guardian angel or spirit, contemplation. Caution. Voice of conscience. Examining the past.
↓ Isolation, loneliness, withdrawal, retirement, depression, asceticism, forgetfulness, obstacle, delay.

AS A PERSON

An elder or older person. A solitary or recluse. A celibate person or widow/er. A time-keeper, referee or expert witness. A historian or archaeologist. A trustworthy person or caretaker. A trusty retainer.

EXAMPLES

- Hermit + Knight of Cups: a wise teacher is pursued by an idealistic follower.
- 4 Batons + Hermit + 3 Swords: your car is getting old and needs to be retired before it breaks down entirely.

A cloaked and hooded elder raises his lantern to peer into the beyond.
His progress is slow, for he is supported by a walking stick. His grave
face and grey hair give him the air of a wise man.

O riginally, the Hermit held an hourglass, signifying that he represented time. He has now lost his hourglass, which over the course of time has changed into a lantern, thereby obscuring his original likeness to Cronos, the god of time. Cronos devours his children and tries to keep things from moving on: the Hermit's association with time is clearly remembered in the *Leber Tarot* of Rouen, where he has the Latin tag, *Rerum Edax*, or "the devourer of time."[36] In Petrarch's *Trionfi*, the Hermit as Time is depicted with wings and crutches, riding upon a chariot drawn by deer: he is the one who overcomes Fame.[37] Significantly, he is situated after the Chariot (representing Fame) and just before the Wheel of Fortune. In this depiction of Time, the Hermit makes his appearance on two crutches, as in the Bolognese-style tarot, where he is sometimes known as Il Gobbo, the Hunchback.

In a reading, this card has a slow or delaying effect and can have a certain inexorable influence over the cards around it, rather like an old person around whom everyone tiptoes. The Hermit takes care and caution to extreme lengths, so check which card the Hermit is illuminating with his lantern. When badly aspected, the wisdom of the Hermit can merely be showing elderly crankiness or just age.

Facsimile Italian Renaissance
Woodcut Tarocchi

X WHEEL OF FORTUNE

None falleth far but he
who climbeth high.

SIR THOMAS MORE, *To Them Who Trust in Fortune*

French: *La Roue de Fortune*
Italian: *La Ruota di Fortuna*
English: *Wheel of Fortune*
Direction: *The wheel turns to the left*

KEYWORDS

↑ Evolution. Cyclic change, sequential patterns. Phases and cycles of time. Luck, lottery, fortune-telling. Rejoicing in your own or another's good fortune. Ambition. Regulation, bureaucracy. Following a course, route or circuit.

↓ Bad luck, devolution, external forces or circumstances out of control, cycles of misfortune, being cast down, *Schadenfreude*, things repeating, failure, unregulated enterprises, going through the motions.

AS A PERSON

Fortune-teller, croupier, gambler, forecaster.

EXAMPLES

- Wheel + 8 Deniers: cash flow is out of phase.
- 2 Batons + Wheel + Hermit: you want to collaborate on a new plan, but you are held in a pattern dictated by time-serving methods.

A great wheel standing upon two plinths spins round as the handle is turned. Upon it are three animals, semi-clothed and with human faces: one struggles to mount the wheel to the top, while another descends to the bottom; at the very top is a crowned beast with a sword and wings, like a winged lion. None of them inspire confidence, and we go away feeling that this is a mockery.

The Wheel of Fortune is an emblem that has permeated Western culture as the symbol of the goddess Fortuna, the mistress of fate and luck. It was frequently applied to rulers as a warning that however high you rise, so too you may fall as the wheel turns. The *Visconti Tarot* shows four figures around the Wheel with the legends against each of them: *Regnabo* – I will reign; *Regno* – I reign; *Regnavi* – I have reigned; and *Sum Sine Regno* – I am without reign. The *Tarot de Marseille* shows only three semi-clothed animals who are apeing human beings, but the sense is the same. When considering the cartomantic pips, I have applied these four phases of the Wheel to the four suits of the pips. (See page 108.)

Cycles of time and phases of life are revealed by the Wheel. The illusion of fortune tells us that we will be all right and that we will reach the summit of our ambition, while we also know, in the same instant, that things will go wrong again and that we will slide down the heap. Fortune beckons and promises much, which is why gamblers always feel that the next trick will be the one.

In a reading, you can check what is turning the handle of the wheel by looking to the card to the right of the Wheel: this is often an instigator of the action playing out, or is the factor that is keeping the Wheel on an adverse cycle of repetition. New phases are often indicated by the card to the left of the Wheel, as an influence that is trying to assert itself.

LA FORCE

Giacomo Zoni Tarot

— XI FORTITUDE —

Above all the grace and the gifts that Christ gives to his beloved is that of overcoming self.

ST FRANCIS OF ASSISI, *I Fioretti*

French: *La Force*
Italian: *La Forza*
English: *Strength*
Esoteric: *Appears at position VIII*
Direction: *Right*

KEYWORDS

↑ Enduring strength, fortitude, the courage to withstand challenges, perseverance. Controlling urges, self-discipline, restraint. Moral strength, physical resilience. Firmly resolved. Expertise, mastery. Being yourself. Daring, bravery and winning through.

↓ Weakness, self-doubt, lack of self-discipline, giving into urges, forceful dominance, over-controlled, doing violence to yourself. A bad piece of work, mangling something. Audacity, manipulation.

AS A PERSON

A manager, troubleshooter, trainer, coach, survivor, a wrangler, animal trainer, a hero.

EXAMPLES

- Fortitude + Ace of Swords: taking up a new way of thinking with courage.
- 5 Batons + Fortitude + Sun: competitiveness gives you the edge to succeed.

A woman in a wide-brimmed hat topped by a crown is fearlessly
subduing a lion. One of her hands is calmly opening the lion's
jaws, while the beast itself sits obediently between her knees.
Her naked right foot braces against the rough ground as
she manoeuvres and tames the lion.

The Cardinal Virtue of Fortitude was originally depicted on many Italian tarots with a column that she was in the process of breaking, like Samson in the temple of Dagon, while in the *Visconti Tarot* this card shows Hercules clubbing the Nemean Lion. The name Fortitude is not the same as Strength, as the latter reduces the enduring resilience of the virtue to a mere strong-arm act, which it is not. The French, *La Force*, also doesn't translate literally into English, where "force" is about violent or coercive manipulation. Anciently, Fortitude was about resisting urges and impulses, enabling moral courage to determine outcomes rather than violence, overcoming animal nature with the highest skills of humanity. Today, Fortitude has turned into a weary or dogged kind of virtue, with gritted teeth, but we still admire those who withstand and overcome the odds to be victorious, whether they survive physical or moral challenges.

In a reading, Fortitude attempts to control or withstand the card to its right. Fortitude shows us dealing with conditions on the ground, about how we maintain ourselves in difficult circumstances without becoming overwhelmed by passions that make animals of us. Occasionally you see someone looking into the lion's mouth, either for a dare or because they are without any protection. Ill-aspected, it may show you biting off more than you can chew.

— XII HANGED MAN —

He by the heels him hung upon a tree,
And baffl'd so, that all which passed by
The picture of his punishment might see.

EDMUND SPENSER, *The Faerie Queene*

French: *Le Pendu*
Italian: *L'Appeso, Il Traditore, L'Impiccato*
English: *The Hanged Man*
Direction: *Faces forward*

Minchiate Florentine

KEYWORDS

↑ A time of purification or purgatory. Hiatus, waiting, delay, procrastination. Self-sacrifice, devotion. Sticking to your agenda, bound by obligations, painted into a corner. Exclusion, exile. Starting out on the wrong foot. Penniless.

↓ Martyrdom. Indecision, sitting on the fence. Deception, betrayal. Passing the buck, blaming others. Torture. Being in the frame, being found guilty. A scapegoat. Punishment. Ostricization. Notoriety. Being pilloried.

AS A PERSON

A traitor or betrayer, a criminal or wrongdoer, a prisoner.
A martyr, someone who suffers or dines out on misfortune.

EXAMPLES

• Hanged Man + Lovers: an affair that never develops.
• The 8 Swords above the Hanged Man, with Popess below: your mental health is becoming of great concern now because you've been silent for too long.

From a roughly hewn set of posts is a strung a man,
hanging by his left foot. Dressed in a parti-colored tunic,
he has his hands bound behind his back and he calmly faces forward.
On either side the supporting posts have six bleeding boughs.

The original image of the Hanged Man of the tarot is based upon the Florentine custom of portraying traitors on placards on the wall of a municipal building as an awful warning to the would-be malefactor, and as a point of information to aggrieved citizens.[38] If the traitor had been caught, he was painted on the wall as being hanged by the neck. But if the traitor was still at large, he was shown being hanged from one heel, in a kind of "wanted" poster. It is in this latter form that we are used to seeing the Hanged Man. What we are really looking at is the image of *someone who has escaped* and who has not yet been brought to judgement. In the *Mitelli Tarocchino*, we see instead the grisly ancient punishment of a nail being hammered through the prisoner's temple by an executioner. Hanging by the feet after execution was the punishment meted out in 1945 to the dictator Benito Mussolini, his mistress Clara Petacci, and other fascists. The figure of the traitor is spurned and scapegoated in all cultures, with the traitor's name living on in infamy from Judas to Ganelon, in the *Song of Roland*, who sold out the Paladins of Charlemagne to the Moors.

As one of the forward-facing trumps, the Hanged Man asks, "What are the demands of your destiny? What is being asked of you?" It leads to a momentous time of decision in which there seems little real choice, where sacrifice is required, as a consent to deeper change. Sometimes the Hanged Man symbolizes people stuck with their own agenda or preoccupied with fulfilling a fate that they decide, or have been told, exists, or still bound by obligations and inconvenient decisions formed in expedience. The Hanged Man can also lead you to consider your guilt or worthiness: suspended between heaven and earth, you belong nowhere, so it is also the card of exclusion or exile. You can lay a card above and below the Hanged Man to check the dynamic of the card: the card above shows the issue you need to face, while the card below is the issue that has been holding things up. In some tarots, the Hanged Man is depicted as Judas, and has money falling from his pockets, giving us the meaning of being "penniless."

Minchiate Florentine

— XIII DEATH —

My life was hardly less than bitter, then,
Compared to the sweet kindliness of death
Vouchsafed to me and rarely to mankind.

PETRARCH, *The Triumph of Death*

French: *Unnamed*
Italian: *Il Morte*
English: *Death*
Direction: *Right*

KEYWORDS

↑ Endings, cancellation, termination, cessation. Ruthless yet compassionate action. Liberation, freedom. Transition. Separation, division, closure. Harvest. Back to basics, essential matters. Clearing away.

↓ Resistance to change, unable to move on. Stagnation. Mortality, death, bereavement. A stark or uncompromising truth, things are stripped bare.

AS A PERSON

Loss assessor, mortician, farmer, forensic scientist, gardener, surgeon, refuse collector.

EXAMPLES

- Death + 8 Swords = stalemate.
- Moon + Death + Page of Deniers: you are fearful that you will lose your material possessions.

A fearsome skeleton with a scythe reaps the dark earth, cutting down
the highborn and the lowborn alike. None escape his scythe, but are
harvested in their due time. His left foot still bears flesh and his right foot
sinks into the dark earth, from which hands and feet protrude in grisly
testimony to his work.

Death appears as the third *Trionfi* of Petrarch, borne upon a chariot drawn by oxen that runs headlong over countless dead bodies. Death conquers Chastity in Petrarch, for it took away his beloved Laura.[39] The headlong and unstoppable progress of death came to prominence during the Black Death of the mid 14th century, when the Grim Reaper harvested an estimated 40–60 per cent of the European population, so it is hardly surprising that Death took its own place in the tarot. In early tarot, Death was often shown on horseback and partially fleshed, later becoming the bare skeleton seen in most tarots. The certainty of death was often depicted in murals or exhibited as a bare skull in a public gathering, as in the old Roman triumphs where someone was employed to remind the victor *momento mori*, or to "be mindful of death." These reminders sought to bring humility to our actions and to stimulate our consciences to perform good deeds before death.

Death thus not only reminds us to be grateful for the power and opportunities of life, but also enables us to accede to "the sweet kindliness of death," as Petrarch calls it; for, when life is no longer possible, we can make an end with grace. Nearly everyone has seen a film where a taromancer lays the Death card as a meme signalling some fatality in the script, so that querents now have a fear of their own death when this card emerges. In a reading, Death is most often about needing to let go of something, make an end and move on. Where it speaks of physical death, it more often speaks of a loss that the querent has recently experienced. If there is something that needs to be cut out or removed, then look at the card facing the scythe. If the question concerns something that is near its end, then the card at Death's back currently has life in it. I remember at the time of the turn of the millennium, when I laid cards about this event's impact on the world, that Death faced the Wheel, saying, most succinctly, "death of an era."

XIIII

TEMPERANCE

CBD Tarot de Marseille

— XIV TEMPERANCE —

Temperance is a most beautiful virtue enabling us to moderate the corporeal pleasures ... without fearing the assaults of Death nor Fortune's inconstancy.

FRANCESCO PISCINA,
Discourse on the Order of the Tarot Figures,
translated by Caitlín Matthews

French: *La Temperance*
Italian: *La Temperanza*
English: *Temperance*
Direction: *Left*

KEYWORDS

↑ Moderation, controlling appetites and desires, self-restraint. Good measure, sufficiency. Balance. Reconciliation, integration, fusion, mediation. Adaptability. Blending, combining, mixing. Medication. Modesty, patience. Good regulation or flow, health. Sobriety. Voice of conscience.
↓ Imbalance, excess, going to extremes, lack of long-term vision, over-medicating, addiction, drunkenness, hedonism, licenciousness.

AS A PERSON

A brewer, wine-maker, a crofter or any self-sufficient profession, a regulator.

EXAMPLES

- Temperance + 10 Deniers: reining back fraudulent transactions.
- Tower + Temperance + 2 Batons: after the crash, it's time to get cleaned up and seek some practical help.

A beautiful angel stands pouring fluid from one vessel into another, with not a drop spilt. The fluid is conveyed so skillfully that it remains in the vessels, no matter how many times it is poured. The angel's wings are spread and on its brow is a five-petalled flower. Its left arm is higher than its right.

Temperance is one of the Cardinal Virtues which enables a person to moderate their pleasures, appetites and desires without being overcome by them. The pouring of water into wine was essential in ancient times when wine was brewed to full strength: Alexander and his Macedonian army often drank undiluted wine, whose potency frequently caused brawls, but his relative Callisthenes was a man of restraint, who always watered his wine and so was acclaimed as a man of principle. In the celebration of the Mass, water and wine are mixed together to acclaim the two natures of Christ, after the dictum by St Athanasius that "God became man so that man might become God." Thus, Temperance reveals how two things can become one through the art of reconciliation and mediation.

In our own times, Temperance is the least heeded of the virtues. In a reading, Temperance reveals what is appropriate or fitting and, when ill-aspected, it shows what is out of balance or simply too much: the card to her left shows the particular tendency or urge, whereas the card to her right shows how to deal with it. Similarly, in a case of dispute, Temperance can reconcile the cards on either side of it or show how matters can be bridged.

— XV DEVIL —

Vandenborre Tarot

*Hell hath no limits, nor is circumscribed
In one self-place; for where we are is hell,
And where hell is, there must we ever be.*

CHRISTOPHER MARLOWE, *Dr Faustus*

French: *Le Diable*
Italian: *Il Diavolo*
English: *The Devil*
Direction: *Faces forward*

KEYWORDS

↑ Force majeure, war. Fear. Challenge, obstacles. Ignorance, mob rule. Limitation. Doomed to repeat your mistakes. Temptation, self-delusion. Collusion in evil, dependency, self-sabotage. Pornography, bondage, entanglement.

↓ Detachment, breaking free, power reclaimed, cleaning up your lifestyle, release from fear. Returning from an unprincipled regime or phase of life.

AS A PERSON

A devil's advocate, a pimp, a subversive, an anarchist, a terrorist, a Machiavelli who plays on your weak points.

EXAMPLES

- Devil + 9 Swords: violent deeds, torture, mental cruelty.
- 9 Deniers + Devil + 4 Batons: the payout on your car is limited.

A dual-sexed being with both exterior genitalia and breasts pokes out his tongue at us. Upon his head are goats' ears and antlers; outspread on his back are bats' wings. His hands and feet are clawed like a cat's. In his left hand is a flaming torch, with which he presides over a pair of naked humans, who have cats' ears and antlers on their heads, and tails, for they have already begun to transform. Together, the humans exchange a collusive look, being tethered to the being's podium by ropes around their necks.

Very few depictions of the Devil remain from ancient tarots, as they were frequently destroyed by successive generations out of superstitious fear or, as we have seen, removed and used in spellcraft. The *Leber Tarot* has an unusual depiction of the Devil as Plutus abducting Persephone, with the Latin tag *Perditorum Raptor,* or "ravisher of the lost."[40] But most tarots show the Devil conventionally as half-animal, half-humanoid – a monster who represents that which we most fear. In the 14th and 15th centuries, the Duomo of Florence and San Pedronio in Bologna had some of the most fearsome depictions of devils. The Devil is used by the Church as the ultimate threat against unprincipled behavior.

In our own time, the exteriorization of evil as the Devil is rarer, and he has been seen as just a bogeyman by the non-religious. Yet evil is nonetheless present in many forms, such as persuasive media statements that play on our ignorance and fear to create mob rule. In his *Dialogue of Comfort Against Tribulation*, Sir Thomas More wrote about how the best antidote to combat the temptations and promptings of the Devil is humor: "the devil, that proud sprite, cannot endure to be mocked." The alternative route to More's solution is to place something stronger than temptation near to you, to get away free and unentangled. It is our own pride that most often keeps us trapped.

In a reading, the Devil usually flags up what the querent is bound to by fear, collusion or self-sabotage. Because it is one of the five forward-facing trumps, you can lay one card over it and another under it: the card above shows what the fear leads to, and the card below helps you to track it to its source.

Giacomo Zoni Tarot

— XVI TOWER —

Do you wish to rise? Begin by descending.
You plan a tower that will pierce the clouds?
Lay first the foundation of humility.

ST AUGUSTINE, *Sermons*

French: *La Maison Dieu, La Foudre*
Italian: *La Torre, La Saetta, Il Fuoco*
English: *The Tower*
Direction: *The Tower's top falls to the left*

KEYWORDS

↑ Shocking change, trauma, upheaval. Act of God. Loss of cosy security. Physical collapse, financial crash. A disaster, an accident. The unavoidable. Homelessness, destitution, exile. Destruction, downfall. Prison break.

↓ Avoidance of disaster, fear of change. Transfiguration, shapeshifting. Coming back from disaster or collapse. Shoring up something that has been condemned.

AS A PERSON

Agony aunt, a doomster, risk assessor, ambulance chaser, demolition merchant.

EXAMPLES

- Tower + Death: a natural disaster.
- 4 Swords + Tower + King of Deniers: a sick employee is facing a shock sacking on return to work because the boss has his mind on lost revenue.

A tall tower is struck by lightning, which causes brilliant balls of light to brighten the sky as the crenellations tumble. Falling from the tower are two individuals, who hit the ground at speed. At the tower's base are two footprints: Can they have been set there by the founder of the tower? We cannot say, for no one lives to tell us.

The destruction of the Tower may be resonant with the fall of many a city from Sodom and Babel to the fall of Jerusalem or the sack of Rome: all great civilizations that were suddenly brought low. But the ultimate location may be suggested by the *Florentine Minchiate*, which shows the expulsion of Adam and Eve from the Garden of Eden through a fiery doorway: in whichever happy or prosperous place we find ourselves, the Tower can expel us from that state. The Tower is what insurance companies mean when they say they will not pay out "in the event of force majeure or Act of God" – for these are circumstances that are unavoidable.

This trump has the greatest number of alternative names in tarot: the French *La Maison Dieu* or "House of God" is hard to understand since, in French, this represents a hospital or pilgrim hostel: expulsion from shelter would be the most merciless action. The alternative names of lightning, *Foudre*, and arrow, *Saetta*, refer to the thunderstruck effect that this card conveys.

When the Tower represents a person, they can appear like the Ancient Mariner, someone who dines out on disasters, or an ambulance chaser, who feeds on the misfortunes of others. When the Tower shows an action, look to its right to see any warning signs about what might bring it on.

Playing Marseille

— XVII STAR —

*The soul exists partly in eternity
and partly in time.*

MARSILIO FICINO,
Commentary on Plato's Symposium

French: *Le Toille*
Italian: *Le Stelle*
English: *The Star*
Direction: *Left*

KEYWORDS

↑ Hope. Vision. Inspiration. Faith. Generosity, love of another's benefit, benefaction, blessing. Refreshment, simplicity. Back to nature. Transmission. Help. Prophecy. The soul.

↓ Lack of faith, despair, discouragement, over-exposure, wishful thinking, gilding the lily, complicating things unnecessarily. Neglect of the soul.

AS A PERSON

Generous friend. A donor or benefactor. Muse or daimon. The emergency services.

EXAMPLES

- Star + Judgement: the preparation that you've made bears fruit.
- 6 Batons + Star + Sun: a university receives a benefaction of brilliance.

As a bird sings its twilight song upon a bush, the first stars begin to stud the brightening sky, with one that shines more piercingly than the others. Beside the gently trickling stream a naked maiden draws up water in two vessels and pours them, one upon the ground, one into the waters, mercifully and gladly. Some things return to night's merciful forgetfulness, while others are refreshed, ready to awaken at morning.

After the fearful cards of the Devil and Tower, it is a relief to turn to the Star. The Star itself is depicted with eight points, which would make it the star of Ishtar or Venus. However, the maiden depicted on the card may be another goddess entirely. The French title, *Le Toille*, is also a *double entendre* for *toile*, "web" or "toil" – a kind of linen or canvas fabric upon which things can be painted or printed, which is how the heavens have been seen, as a great tapestry reflecting the ages. In Neoplatonic myth, Persephone represents the soul. Just before her abduction to Hades, she was said to be weaving a scarf for her mother. Claudian's *De Raptu Prosperpina* tells us, "In this cloth she embroidered with her needle the concourse of atoms and the dwelling of the Father of the gods and pictured how Mother Nature ordered elemental chaos."[41] In his elemental system, the Pre-Socratic philosopher Empedocles wrote of Persephone as Nestis, the goddess of water: "Now harken to the fourfold roots of everything: enlivening Hera (earth), Hades (fire), shining Zeus (air), and Nestis (water), moistening mortal springs with her tears."[42] Which is why we may be viewing Persephone, rather than Venus. The *Leber Tarot* shows the Star with the Latin tag *Inclitum Sydus*, or "glorious star."[43]

The *Viéville Tarot* shows an astrologer with dividers, while in the *Tarocchino Bolognese* tradition the Star trump depicts the Star of Bethlehem, as followed by the Three Magi, which gives the card its Bolognese meaning of "gift." In the Basilica of St Pedronio, Bologna, the Chapel of the Magi was decorated with frescos in about 1420 by Giovanni da Modena, creating the iconography for this card. In a reading, the Star brings hope and new vision, enabling us to see helpful ways through.

— XVIII MOON —

Vergnano Tarot

That which is above the moon, they call the region of the pious, because they believe souls live there after leaving their bodies. But they call that sublunary region, where all living things are fallen, the infernal realm.

MARTIANUS CAPELLA,
De Nuptiis Philologiae et Mercurii

French: *La Lune*
Italian: *La Luna*
English: *The Moon*
Direction: *Left*

KEYWORDS

↑ Dreams and visions. Emotions. Your inner condition. Anxieties and niggling little fears. Flow. Subconscious understandings. Strangers and foreigners. Uncertainty, mutability, gradual change. Night and nocturnal matters.

↓ Illusions, ebbing, nightmares, suspicions and suppositions, a growth, vagueness.

AS A PERSON

Psychological therapist, scout, spiritualist, psychic, navigator.

EXAMPLES

• Sun + Moon: pleasure and sorrow are mixed together.
• Queen of Batons + Moon + Knight of Batons: your friend is being a drama queen and her nightmare scenario will look less scary when you give her some confident help.

*Night's dark has fallen, changing the interior condition of the psyche;
a strange landscape is illuminated by a hypnotic crescent moon, inviting
you into a terrain where no boundary is safe or fixed. Whether by land
or water, you have to traverse the unknown, shifting as best you can
where reason no longer has sway. Between two towers two canines bay
at the moon, and, in the depths of the lake, a crayfish can be seen.*

T he card contains a rebus that only makes sense if you speak French. The
two canines baying at the moon are a rebus of *entre chien et loup*, or
"between dog and wolf," an expression that is used of twilight when colors
become indistinguishable from each other; this is also how the start of the
Jewish Sabbath is defined. This rebus reveals something about the nature of
the card: under the influence of the moon we sometimes cannot determine one
thing from another. In this indeterminate space we fall into surmise or super-
stition in which inchoate fears arise. On Ferrarese tarots, these anxieties are
shown by the placement of a spinning woman as an emblem of fate, whose
spindle represents that of the Moirae.

In the Middle Ages the region between the moon and the earth was regarded
as the sublunary realm, meaning that everything on earth was subject to the
moon's influence. We know that this is scientifically borne out in the cycles of
growth and the tides of the sea, as well as in triggering many other physical
changes in animals, plants and humans. The sublunary regions were believed to
be separated from the celestial or heavenly zone, and so the earth was subject
to change and mutability.

The Moon in a reading gives three levels of images to work with: the moon
itself may be shining upon what is important in your dreams, while the dogs
may be bringing to your attention what you need to understand better. The
crayfish may be showing you what is triggering your anxieties. Try reading the
cards either side like a tapestry that stretches from tower to tower, leading you
through this temporary uncertainty, or lay out three cards vertically to correspond to the moon as the influence, the land as the terrain you are traveling
through, and the water as what is still unknown.

Facsimile Italian Renaissance Woodcut Tarocchi (note Ferrarese numeration here)

— XIX SUN —

What sweetness is left in life,
if you take away friendship?
Robbing life of friendship is like
robbing the world of the sun.
A true friend is more to be esteemed
than kinsfolk.

MARCUS TULLIUS CICERO, *The Laws*

French: *Le Soleil*
Italian: *Il Sole*
English: *The Sun*
Direction: *Faces forward*

KEYWORDS

↑ Day and daytime matters, conscious understanding. Your outer condition and well-being. Reassurance, safety, encouragement. Success. Enthusiasm, warmth, joy, wholeness. Companionship, friendship. Enlightenment, radiance, cheerfulness, happiness. Play, leisure, pleasure.
↓ Temporary depression, lack of success, burnout, mania. Happiness and well-being are restricted in some way. Overcast. A busman's holiday.

AS A PERSON

Siblings, friends, relatives, the community, or people in your life or circle.

EXAMPLES

- Moon + Sun: the bad times are departing, and the good times are coming.
- 6 Cups + Sun + Juggler: your inner circle have a wonderful time at the show.

High in the sky shines the sun, shedding its beams of light upon everyone. Beneath its broad face stands a pair of half-naked children before a low wall. The child on the left reaches towards his fellow, while the one on the right reassures him with one hand upon his shoulder. The child on the right stands on slightly higher ground.

At the time that the tarot was made, in a pre-Galileo and pre-Copernican era, the Sun was not seen as the center of the universe, for the early 15th-century world still believed in the Ptolemaic system in which the Earth is the planet around which every celestial body turns. In medieval metaphysical systems, the Sun was accorded its place as the emblem of Apollo, who harmonizes all things. In the *Tarocchino Bolognese*, the Sun depicts a woman with a distaff: this image may be lost on us today, because we no longer understand that spinning was a task that could only be done while the light was good, so you spun while the sun shone, from dawn to dusk, thereby making the distaff an emblem of daylight. In the Ferrarese decks, a youth – probably Apollo – runs with the sun upon his head, while in the Belgian *Vandenborre Tarot* the youth is on a horse holding a red-cross flag attached to a pennant – an image that finally reappeared in the *Rider Waite-Smith Tarot*.

The two children shown in the *Tarot de Marseilles*, Paul Huson suggests, are derived from an understanding of the fifth astrological house, which is governed by the Sun and concerns children and pleasures, which were often depicted as two children playing.[44]

As one of the cards that faces forward, the Sun assures you that it shines also upon you, and that all good things that you would wish for in your life stand near at hand. See which cards touch the Sun on any of its edges: it can shed light on what is uncertain in these cards and bring encouragement, or it can de-escalate situations that are getting too serious.

— XX JUDGEMENT —

Vergnano Tarot

To you is granted the power, contained within your intellect and judgement, to be reborn into the higher forms, the divine.

GIOVANNI PICO DELLA MIRANDOLA,
Oratio de Hominis Diginitate

French: *Le Jugement*
Italian: *L'Angelo*
English: *(The Last) Judgement*
Direction: *Faces forward*

KEYWORDS

↑ Regeneration, renewal, resurrection, restoration, re-membering, reincarnation. Recapitulation or recycling. A final outcome, day of reckoning, resolution. Ancestral healing. A wake-up call, conversion, turning point. Vocation.

↓ Self-doubt, refusal to self-examine, unavoidable scrutiny. Everything hidden or secret is discovered. Postponement. Under sentence. Forgetfulness, recalcitrant.

AS A PERSON

Whistle-blower, ancestors, readjuster, missionary, ordinand. A zombie.

EXAMPLES

- Judgement + Emperor: a new era is dawning with the election of a leader.
- Judgement with 8 Batons above and 5 Deniers below: being called out of your safe little space to do your real work.

From a cloud door in the heavens, in a blaze of glory, the announcing
angel with outspread wings calls the dead to rise from their tombs by
means of a trumpet, on which flies a flag with a cross. Men, women and
children, old and young, good and bad, arise at the call.

In Italy this card is known simply as "the Angel," for it comes on Doomsday to waken the sleepers from wherever they have been buried. All Catholics believed in the physical reconstitution of dead bodies on Judgement Day, when the entirety of a person would be judged, body and soul, according to their deeds. Judgement is second in the Catholic doctrine of *the Four Last Things* – Death, Judgement, Heaven and Hell – that determine the destination of the awakened dead. (See page 179.) This trump is customarily depicted, as here, with the dead being called from their tombs: we see the moment before the souls, with their bodies, become glorified in Heaven, are damned to Hell or are to be purified in Purgatory.

In an era in which the prospect of the Final Judgement fails to bring terror, this trump can come as a wake-up call or literal "last trump" in a reading. Sleepers awake, re-membering what they had forgotten, as all is reckoned up and judged. For some, it will bring a conversion of their lives or spiritual path, or a chance to regenerate, heal or restore. This is my favorite trump, for it calls us to change and learn about our higher nature, to fulfill our soul's promise. Because it is one of the forward-facing cards, we know that the trumpet sounds also for us, and so you can place a card over Judgement to see what you are being called to, and place another beneath it to see the nature of the tomb you are in.

CBD Tarot de Marseille

— XXI WORLD —

I saw the sun, the heavens, and the stars
And land and sea unmade, and made again
More beauteous and more joyous
than before.

PETRARCH, *The Triumph of Eternity*

French: *Le Monde*
Italian: *Il Mondo*
English: *The World*
Direction: *To the left*

KEYWORDS

↑ Completion, culmination, attainment, perfection, conclusion. Androgyny. World Soul, eternity, universal. Opportunities open up, a world view or outlook. Life itself, a long journey. Becoming part of the whole.

↓ Lack of completion, being put in your place, stuck in a world not of your choosing, waiting to break out or leave home. A painfully won independence.

AS A PERSON

Travel agent, a guide, dancer. Mr or Mrs Worldly Wiseman.

EXAMPLES

• Knight of Swords + World: saving the world.
• Queen of Deniers + World + Wheel: the opportunity to spin the roulette wheel of international investment.

*A garland of laurel leaves appears in the sky and, dancing within it,
standing on its right foot, is a naked being, bearing in its left hand a
wand. A narrow red scarf encircles this being, so that it is not possible
to distinguish its sex. Framing the garland in each direction are four
fabulous creatures. Above the being's head are an angel and an eagle.
Below its feet are an ox and a lion.*

This image of the World shows us a mandorla of leaves in which the resurrected Christ in glory stands. In the four corners of the card are the Four Holy Living Creatures from Ezekiel, who here appear with the attributes of the four Evangelists: the angel or man of St Matthew; the eagle of St John; the bull of St Luke; and the lion of St Mark. In Petrarch's sixth and final *Trionfi*, Eternity triumphs over Time, depicted by the Holy Trinity borne upon a chariot.[45]

The World is truly universal in application, for it signifies the World Soul, the Anima Mundi. It is the visual inverse of the Hanged Man: for while both are framed, the Hanged Man stands on his left foot and the World on its right, but the correct way up. In the *Rosenwald Minchiate, Visconti* and *Gringonneur* tarots, we see a globe in which a microcosm is shown: in the *Gringonneur* and *Rosenwald* cards, this globe has a haloed angel standing upon it, with orb and sceptre signifying the virtue of Prudence.

In a reading, the World may show you that the world is your oyster, or even that the world is what you make of it. Wherever we go, however we see it, we cannot be separate from the world, although each individual defines the world differently and this colors their outlook. It is interesting to see what the World looks at to the left, for it gives you some idea of what the querent's world view is like; the untold possibilities lie to the right of the card.

TRUMPS AS INDICATORS

In a reading, you will often find that the trumps speak about different aspects of life, such as periods in a person's life, rites of passage, or of motion and pace. Consider these indicators, especially when they appear next to a face or court card:

RITES OF PASSAGE	
XIX Sun	Birth
0 Fool	Gap year
XXI World	Leaving home
VII Chariot	Graduation
VI Lovers	Marriage
III Empress	Motherhood
IV Emperor	Fatherhood
IX Hermit	Old age/retirement
MOTION AND PACE	
VII Chariot	Fast
IX Hermit	Slow, having to go back on things
X Wheel	Retrograde/fast forward
XII Hanged Man	Delay
XIII Death	Stop
XVI Tower	Down/fall
XX Judgement	Up or returning
XXI World	A felicitous journey
0 Fool	An unfortunate journey

SEQUENTIAL PAIRINGS

When trumps come together they often form powerful combinations, but when certain pairs appear together in their sequential order, these are epoch-changing moments on the cusp of becoming.

Vulnerable people need to be aware of this pairing. The Juggler sees the Fool coming, and how he might be manipulated or taken advantage of.

Popess + Empress Can express female solidarity or, if badly aspected, show a divergence of female values, such as between a single and a married woman, or clashes between career and home, utility and elegance, or academic and vocational work.

Emperor + Pope When temporal and spiritual powers combine or face off, there are often wars, social unrest and upheaval in the world. As with the Popess and Empress, this male pair can show a strategic coming together of different male values or an argument over them. It can signify a collusion, where political expedience is egged on by religious values.

Pope + Lovers A traditional combination speaking of a marriage or contract. Equally, it might reveal a religious interference in a relationship.

Chariot + Justice The Chariot's speed meets the law's delay here; this pairing reveals someone in a tearing hurry to get to the truth.

Hermit + Wheel Here, the slowness of the Hermit meets the unexpected movement of the Wheel. Expect time-collapses and elisions as things speed up suddenly: all the time that you thought you had vanishes.

Wheel + Fortitude This speaks of a cycle or phase that you must endure.

Hanged Man + Death This is a traditional pairing that signifies someone getting a just punishment for their deeds; it still represents capital punishment.

Temperance + Devil Despite all urgings and good advice to the contrary, someone is taking the road to ruin. This is also the traditional combination for poisoning.

Tower + Star When these two cards come together, we can expect to see an epoch-making change around the topic under consideration.

Moon + Sun These cards together signify day and night on one level, but they also signify, in *Tarocchino Bolognese* tradition, displeasure that passes. When the Sun precedes the Moon, it is showing a trouble that doesn't pass away, or a mixture of joy and sorrow.

Judgement + World Something immense is being announced to the world at large. This could herald the return of a movement, or an idea that becomes current in the everyday world.

CHAPTER 3

THE TALKATIVE PIPS

❦

In the shuffling of the cards, smell the earth a-growing,
In the pattering of the cards, see the rain a-falling.
In the beating of the cards, feel the cold wind a-blowing,
In the pointing of the cards, hear the fire's ancient call.

CAITLÍN MATTHEWS, *Tarot Chant*

SUIT ORIGINS

Tarot suits seem to have originated from playing cards such as the 15th-century *Mamluk* cards, the Arabic forerunners of Western playing cards and tarot pips. A set of *Mamluk* cards was found in the library of the Topkapi Palace in Istanbul by L.A. Mayer who wrote a study on them in 1939.[46] In their turn, these *Mamluk* cards may have stemmed from prototype playing cards made in China. The *Mamluk* deck, called *Mulūk wa-nuwwāb* (or Kings and Viceroys), is a pack of fifty-two cards, of which only forty-one remain. Its four suits of coins, polo sticks, cups and scimitars are recognizable in Italian and Spanish decks, except that the polo sticks have become Batons. In each suit, there are ten numerical cards and three courts: king, viceroy and second viceroy. The clinching evidence is that, in Spain, which was itself Moorish for seven hundred years, playing cards are still called *naipes* after *nā'ib*, the Arabic word for "viceroy."[47] Here are the names of the *Mamluk* suits and how they have flowed into tarot and playing cards:

TAROT SUITS	PLAYING CARDS	MAMLUK EMBLEMS
Swords	Spades	*Suyūf* or Scimitars
Batons	Clubs	*Jawkān* or Polo Sticks
Cups	Hearts	*Tūmān* or Cups (literally "multitudes")
Deniers	Diamonds	*Darāhim* or Coins

The nature of the tarot suits is shared with the playing card suits and there is considerable flow between them. Even today, Italian playing cards still retain the Knights along with the Pages, Queens and Kings. French suited cards with hearts, diamonds, spades and clubs came in during the 15th century, while in Switzerland and Germany the playing card suits are hearts, bells, acorns and leaves; however, these cards have no Queen, merely an under-Knave, an over-Knave and a King.

Medieval Italian tarot users already recognized the symbology of the tarot as an everyday experience: the Chariot was a triumphal float, a man hanging from one foot was a traitor, the Wheel of Fortune was what happened when you strove to get above your allotted position in life. They recognized that Deniers were money, that Swords were strife, that Batons were staves of office or strength, and that Cups were pleasure. They didn't worry about the esoteric meanings of tarot because these hadn't yet been invented. It is clear from examining earlier sources from the 16th century that the suits were understood to govern the following areas[48] (here, we also see the Italian and French suit names and their 16th-century Italian associations):

ITALIAN	FRENCH	ASSOCIATION
Spade	*Épées*	Military Power
Mazzo	*Batons*	Political Power
Coppe	*Coupes*	Gluttony and Pleasure
Denari	*Deniers*	Riches

When Court de Gébelin and Comte de Mellet were intent on creating their speculative esoteric origins for the tarot, they built on these earlier meanings, but associated the four suits with the four estates of society, with Swords for the military, Batons for farming peasants, Cups for the Church, and Deniers for merchants.[49] Another way of understanding the suits is to look at their actual actions, where we find obvious connections and meaning in the function of each suit emblem, suggesting their actions, and the possible overspill of the suits' powers into the court cards.

Swords Strike, defend, clash and define. As people they can be sharply astute, defensive.

Batons Fence, combine, burn and grow. As people they can overwhelm, become ardent.

Cups   Hold, nurture, spill and contain. As people they can be
emotional, indulgent.

Deniers Manifest, spend, save and hoard. As people they can be cautious,
pragmatic.

These are the literal actions arising from each of the emblems: most standardized tarot meanings derive from the physical actions or properties of the suit
emblems. Both Swords and Batons were considered to be "long suits" by those
using historical decks, while Cups and Deniers were seen as the "round suits":
these descriptive titles were based wholly on their appearance.[50] Modern users
have been encouraged in recent books to view the long suits as "hard" and the
round suits as "soft."[51] The Swords and Batons are now understood to be more
harsh or active in their effect than the Deniers and Cups, much as the black
suits in playing cards are seen as more challenging than the red suits.

The historic view of the pips has varied over time. A 1650 French text of
rules for reading pips bluntly tells us: "… from the ten to the ace, these cards
bear no small resemblance to the dregs of society, people who are much more
a burden than a pleasure."[52] While Paulmy d'Argenson, writing in France in
1779, says of the suits: "The general rules are as follows: the hearts indicate
happiness and success in gallantry, and the diamonds, of one's interests and
finance; clubs are favorable to one's ambitious views, and spades to war
projects or military advancement: when contrary, the spades are unfavorable
in the affairs of gallantry, the clubs must give reason to fear that financial
and business interests go wrong, the hearts announce great disappointment
in projects of ambition, and the diamonds act contrary to soldiers. If it is a
married man who questions and is distinguished, the king is the most favorable card there is, if it is a woman, then it is the queen; and if it is a young
person, it is the Valet. The tens signify the greatest happiness or misfortune,
then the nines, eights or sevens in the decreasing order, and finally the ace is
the smallest injury or slightest advantage."[53] He sees the pips as of decreasing
in influence from 10 to the Ace; this listing of cards in descending order is
common in historic tarot, though modern tarot books favor ascending order
in their listings.

Paulmy d'Argenson's rules for reading cards tell us also about the four suits
of playing cards:

SUITS	FAVORABLE	UNFAVORABLE
Spades (Swords)	To war, conflict	To love
Clubs (Batons)	To ambitions	To plans and finance
Hearts (Cups)	To happiness, love	To ambitions
Diamonds (Deniers)	To projects, money	To soldiers

The Diamonds or Deniers acting "contrary to soldiers" can be understood best by remembering that Diamonds were considered to be the sharp or dangerous suit in cartomancy; while in taromancy, we consider the delayed payment of soldiers, or the inability of mercenaries to retain any cash. It also tells us about the significance of court cards, omitting the Knight, since this card doesn't appear in playing cards.

Despite varying definitions, the pips are generally seen as of having less importance: the 17th-century French text cited opposite is scathing in saying that they represent the *canaille* or riff-raff, not the élite! Pips have remained the poor relation of tarot reading, even being called "the minor arcana" by Paul Christian in 1871, when this term was first coined to suit his Egyptian initiation theory for tarot origins.[54] The pips are usually badly served in most books about historical tarot reading, with scant attention paid to them and a greater emphasis being given to the trumps, so let's look more closely at them now.

APPROACHING THE PIPS

The number cards or pips, as they are colloquially known among card users, initially represent a challenge to tarot readers who are used to illustrated cards. Suddenly, there is no visual cue or prompt to bring out the meaning, only an accumulation of cups, swords, batons and deniers, as we can see overleaf. Instead of the pictorial images of the top row, which closely resemble the *Rider Waite-Smith* style of tarot, the reader is now confronted with its *Tarot de Marseille* equivalent beneath it. Although we can easily identify the trump of the Lovers, the pip cards don't immediately convey visual correlations to the illustrated cards.

When faced with this sudden change, we have to remember that our current familiarity with pictorial number cards in tarot is only just over one hundred years old. Behind that lies nearly six hundred years of lost skill. Our difficulty in reading with non-illustrated pip cards is thus a modern one. In past centuries, there was an understanding of the qualities of each suit and their numbers by those who played card games, as well as by those who read with the ordinary

Moving from Modern to Ancient Tarots.
Top line: *Sharman-Caselli Tarot, 2005*
Bottom line: *Tarot de Marseille Pierre Madenié 1709*

playing card deck. A kind of folk argot about reading the numbers cards grew up across Europe, but it was not a standardized language. Each reader had his own associations or her own preferences, so that every reader would understand the number cards in personal ways. This is demonstrated today in the practice of cartomancy, where a number of standard views are shared, such as an understanding of Spades (the equivalent of the tarot's Swords suit) as being an unlucky or challenging suit; however, individual methods of reading and interpreting cards remain eclectic and non-standard.

We are going to honor that tradition in this book by looking at different ways of reading the number cards. From this variety of approaches, you will be able to build up your own style, based upon your own understandings:

- By seeing visual correlations to the pips from our own understanding.
- By combining suit and number.
- By using cartomantic values derived from the divinatory meanings of playing cards.
- By seeing the pips as the courts of the four Cardinal Virtues. (See Chapter 4.)
- By associating the suits with the functions of our own bodies or with a tree, and the numbers with sequential unfolding.
- By assigning to the pip numbers the themes found in the numbered trumps.
- By reading directionally and sequentially to see the story. (See Chapter 6.)

When faced with the change from pictorial to pip tarots, as shown opposite, the temptation may be to merely translate the pip cards back into your usual pictorial language and treat them exactly the same, but there are problems with this method. The language of pictorial tarots has different values to that of the pip tarots: *Rider Waite-Smith* and the *Tarot de Marseille* come from utterly different eras and backgrounds, and have varying value systems.

The *Rider Waite-Smith Tarot* dates from after the esoteric watershed of the 18th century, with the addition of all the magical symbolism of the Hermetic Order of the Golden Dawn, and the budding psychology of the early 20th century in its background, with images made in the theatrical style of Pamela Coleman Smith, who also designed stage sets. The images, with few exceptions, are shown in a modern humanist style: the people depicted on the trumps are the kinds of people we might easily meet on the street, save for Death. This same humanist style is seen in the *Sharman-Caselli Tarot* opposite.

The *Tarot de Marseille* has its roots in 15th-century Italian tarot design and dates from before the esoteric reinvention of tarot: its trumps still speak the language of Renaissance Europe, with a mixture of Christian and classical ideas, while the court and number cards are based on day-to-day activities. Its pictures and emblems are cut into woodblocks, and the people depicted in the trumps are archetypal beings whom we would no way meet in the street: they come from another world. Only in the court cards or in the trumps of the Fool and Juggler might we see fellow human beings.

We cannot read the early tarots as we read the modern ones. We need to use other, older skills. However, this doesn't mean that we won't be able to read tarot for modern needs and questions: the cards will still speak eloquently to you. I invite you to make the shift into these earlier skills of reading as your ability to read the historic tarots gains fluency; until then, use your own understanding or consult this chapter to keep you on track.

VISUAL PIP READING

We saw how, on page 31, the Pratesi list of *Tarocchino Bolognese* cards reveals the folk argot of tarot reading, with short keywords or titles for the working cards that have arisen from the appearance of the pips on the cards. Here, the Ace of Deniers has become a visual representation of a table, while 10 Deniers is seen as lots of coins, or money. You can also play this game.

Take out your cards and look them over (see below): could 6 Swords be a garden, or a think-tank which fosters growth? Could 2 Cups show an ornamental fountain or a trip to the sea? Does 8 Batons remind you of an impassable fence or a crossroads? And could 8 Deniers be a set of files in which to store facts, a book of many chapters or a dormitory of separate cubicles? This method of visual identification is entirely personal and idiosyncratic, based on associations that you alone make.

For example, while shuffling the other day, the cards exploded into the air, going everywhere, and I lost the Ace of Swords from a very precious tarot. I asked another tarot where it had gone and drew: 9 Swords, 7 Batons, 2 Cups and 5 Deniers (see opposite).

Looking at the cards wholly from a descriptively visual perspective, I noticed that three of these cards have odd numbers, with the one even-numbered card, which shows a stem arising between both cups, sandwiched between them. I understood immediately that the answer was "the card is between two other things." Sure enough, it turned up between two pieces of paper, because

Visual Pips, CBD Tarot de Marseille

| 6 Swords | 2 Cups | 8 Batons | 8 Deniers |

Lost Card, *Tarot de Marseille*
Pierre Madenié 1709

9 Swords

7 Batons

2 Cups

5 Deniers

it had fallen into an open-topped file. From a reading perspective, 9 Swords is a grievous loss to me and, as the top card of this spread, represents me panicking; 7 Batons tells me that the card is between several pieces of paper, and 2 Cups says (from the dolphins on that card) that it has just dived in. 5 Deniers reassures me that the card is quite safe and not lost, secure in its cocoon. This interpretation was drawn solely from the visuals.

Explore this method for yourself by drawing cards in answer to your own questions and see how you can derive visual understanding from your cards. The cards will respond flexibly to different questions so, for example, should 7 Batons recur in another reading, responding to a question about an argument you've had with someone, it might well suggest that a third party could be called in to arbitrate between you and your opponent. The card is the same but the context is different: there is no fixed meaning in this way of reading.

Some readers like to explore the decorative buds, flowers and leaves that grace some pips, finding meaning in them that way. This is an interesting and sometimes helpful practice, if you examine the progress of the foliage when you lay out a sequence of pips. In the *Tarot de Marseille*, the Swords tend to have interior foliage that grows *within* the frame of the swords, but 5, 7, 9 and 10 have only buds; the Batons have exterior foliage which grows *outside* the frame of sticks, although 9 Batons has no foliage whatever. The Cups have the most flowing and exuberant foliage but 10 Cups has none. The Deniers have the most sinuous stalks of all the cards, containing and supporting the coins. However, many pip tarots do not have such helpful prompts, so this cannot become a science that is transferrable between tarots, and I have not found it so useful in my work because I use many different historical packs. So here I will be focusing upon general skills that work for every tarot. You will undoubtedly use a wide range of skills and observations, and don't need to be slavish in sticking to just one criteria. Be prepared to extend your skills over time, be flexible and don't fall into the kind of rigid dogmatism that can bedevil taromancy, whereby you hear someone say, "You can't read 9 Cups like that, it *always* means X."

Cards have their own language and we are going to listen hard to understand the story in as many ways as we can, just like a new language learner who enters a country with a minimum vocabulary: you hear words you can't understand, often in different dialects, and you must watch the eyes and gestures of the speaker to comprehend their intent; you look at the road signs and symbols to steer where you need to go. Yet this very same kind of observation will translate into the way you read cards aloud. You may not have perfect linguistic comprehension yet but, just as a new learner of Italian can request a gelato, ask the way to the Duomo and buy apples in a satisfactory way, with a very few words, so, too, will you be able to unlock the pips. As with all learning, you will need effort, stamina and a preparedness of mind to continue with pip decks: encourage yourself every day to con a little more vocabulary, find a new insight, ask fresh questions of your cards. If you have any lingering sense – after reading illustrated tarot for so many years – that you have been sent, demeaningly, back to school, don't be dismayed: you will be able to develop and learn ways of reading that enrich your approach to taromancy.

PIP NUMBER ASSOCIATIONS

The figure of the tetraktys long held sway as the central philosophical teaching of Pythagoras, showing not only mathematical relationships but also revealing our place in the universe and life's divine creative outpouring. However, in considering how we can read the numbers on the pip cards, there are some basic understandings that arise from our common human experience of numbers:

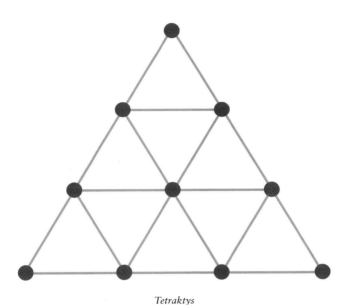

Tetraktys

1 *Beginning, origin, primal principle*

One is the beginning, the source and essence. It is original, one in itself. Most of the Aces stand for the prime principles of life. Ones lead their suits as exemplars and way-showers. Aces show us the spark, seed, instigation, primal impetus, arousal and initial beginnings where things are conceived or initiated.

2 *Partnership, cooperation, conflict, dialogue*

Two is a pair that works together or can face up as opposites. Two can be a dialogue or interface where discussion or argument ensues. Twos are twins that can double things: the power to create a child or to form a friendship. Twos gives us relationship, meetings, responses, attractions; places where transaction and dialogue take place, or where we see the binary of inner/outer, so that we can confirm, affirm and decide.

3 *Creative growth, expansion, abundance, development*
Three is a product of Two and One coming together, so things can expand in a magical way. Three is a creative kernel from which yet more can grow. Threes give us points to see what is emerging, manifesting, growing; the bonds that help in planning, projecting, preparing and creating.

4 *Stability, foundation, rest*
Four is a number of stability: four walls make a house, there are four legs on a mammal, four wheels on a cart or car to keep it upright. Here, things can stabilize or rest securely. Fours give us order, moderation, rigidity, stabilization, conservation and pattern.

5 *Capability, interaction, uncoordinated, discord, strife, illness*
Our head, arms and legs make Five, as well as the five fingers and toes on each hand and foot. What can be thought, wrought or reached by human endeavor is encompassed by Five: our capability to grasp a thing brings us skill but our lack of coordination can lead to discord or illness. When humans clash, there conflict can also flare. Fives give us adapting, changing, dichotomy, crisis, challenge, abrasiveness and divisive struggle.

6 *Harmony, balance, health, social networks, reception*
Six is made up of Two and Four, giving us cooperative stability or harmony. It can also be made from Three and Three, giving us creative growth and abundance as balance or health. What is held in balance can be beneficial all round, shared by many, and so Six can flag up the nature of the environment as network and cooperation. Sixes show us community, charity, mercy and maintenance.

7 *Improvement, luck, opportunity, faith*
Seven is made up of Three and Four, giving us expansive stability or improvement. Seven can give us the turning point we need through the luck of the moment, if we have the faith to cooperate with the opportunity. Sevens explore possibilities, actions, negotiations, and show how perseverance, expanding and experimenting come into things. When we miss the opportunity, we say we have bad luck, so Sevens can also show the doorstep moment when this happened.

8 *Accomplishment, consolidation, re-evaluation, change*

Eight is made up of two Fours; when stability is doubled, we all recognize the manifestation of powerful accomplishment. Eights consolidate but they can also result in restlessness, leading to re-evaluation or change where we refine or make a directional shift. Eights help us to refine choices and re-evaluate, showing us enforced changes or areas where we can shift; they help us to structure, limit or assess our benchmarks.

9 *Wish, ambition, disappointment, rewards, consequences*

Nine is made up of Four and Five, giving us stable interaction or the ability to aspire to even better ideals, taking us to optimum capability. Here, we see both wishes and disappointments manifested in rewards or consequences. Nines reveal how things come to culmination, how they flow, integrate, increase, miss the mark or overspill.

10 *Success, completion, failure, excess*

Ten is made up of Five and Five: doubling activity can create success or failure, completion or excess. The prime principle of the suit expressed by its Ace expands to ultimate expression in the Ten. It cannot go further without beginning again. Tens show the extremity of accumulation or dissolution, where accomplishment brings us to conclusion or where effort has spectacularly failed.

In considering these numbers, we observe that the odd numbers are dynamic points of change and movement, whereas the even numbers are points of holding or stability. The binary relationship of number to number as the cards pair together in a dance can give us platforms from which to read and understand. (See Chapter 5.) If you lay out your pips in ascending or descending order, you will find these dances visually for yourself: the curved scimitars of the Swords create circles, the Batons make a criss-cross fence, while in the Cups and Deniers you will discover how the buds blossom, unfold or die back.

Watch how the numbers rise or fall in a reading: 2 Swords next to 10 Swords reveals a sudden, increasing intensity, while 7 Cups followed by 3 Cups shows a more gradual decrease. When a reading has many of the same numbered cards or many of the same suit, return to this page to explore the theme.

QUALITIES OF THE SUITS

When we set aside the esoteric correlations that have come into the suits from astrology, kabbala and other intruders, we can derive some defining characteristics (see opposite). These characteristics of the suits are not exhaustive, and you will surely find many others, but they give a flavor of each of the suit families.

These qualities can be combined with the numbers to give meaning to each of the pips. *What follows is not fixed in stone, nor are the examples of meanings given the only ones that are possible:* you will find your own combinations as you go. Consider these associations as leaping-off points which, when used to answer a specific question, will unlock other meanings.

We can assign meaning to historic tarot suits using some of the qualities listed below:

Swords   Intellect, rational, verbal, aggressive, sharp, ambition, analytical, decisive, discernment, struggling, belief, seed.
Air, Justice.

Batons   Desire, passionate, outgoing, energetic, creative, sociable, recreative, expressive, impulsive, dominating, volatile, reactive, branch.
Fire, Fortitude.

Cups   Emotions, romantic, relating, sentimental, domestic, devoted, nostalgic, yearning, responsive, intuitive, reservoir.
Water, Temperance.

Deniers   Physical, material, practical, conservative, cautious, grounded, expressive, manifesting, secure, finance, root.
Earth, Prudence.

Overleaf, we will look at each of the pip number and suit combinations in turn.

Opposite: Characteristics of the four suits

CHARACTERISTIC	SWORDS	BATONS	CUPS	DENIERS
Primary quality	Truth	Energy	Compassion	Wisdom
Expressed as	Enforcing justice	Power	Love	Caution
Literal mode	Challenges	Work	Home	Finance
Expressed as	Struggles	Output	Comfort	Gain and loss
Affected by	Destruction	Construction	Healing	Experience
Operating mode	War	Government	Peace	Commonwealth
Expressed as	Defence and attack	Communication	Culture	Order
Operated by	Champion	Governor	Mediator	Coordinator
Physical body	Head	Heart	Soul	Body
Expressed in	Nerves	Blood	Organs	Bones
Functions	Motives	Intuitions	Emotions	Sensations
Actions	Thoughts	Speech	Feelings	Deeds
Relating as	Individual	Peer	Family	Ancestor
Expressed by	Boundaries	Exchanges	Common values	Inherited values
Deals with	Enemies	Friends	Couples	Collectives
By means of	Aggression	Gregariousness	Intimacy	Possession
Values	Independence	Sharing	Generosity	Inheritance
Enjoys	Decisiveness	Organizing	Pleasure	Rewards
Usual mode	Incisive	Passionate	Romantic	Pragmatic
Also	Precise	Dynamic	Artistic	Shrewd
Tendencies	Aggressive	Impulsive	Sentimental	Conservative
Also	Cruel	Forceful	Heartless	Mercenary
Fed by	Ideas	Actions	Beauty	Resources
Culture	Science	Technology	Arts	Humanities
Elemental	Air	Fire	Water	Earth
Expressed in	Atmosphere	Electricity	Tides	Gravity

COMBINING NUMBER AND SUIT KEYWORDS

The examples given here are composed of the number and the suit keywords combined, in that order. Again, they are merely examples, not the *only* meanings that you will find; to remind you of them, I have put the combined words into brackets below. This is the means to a much wider lexicon of pip meanings, whereby you expand your divinatory vocabulary.

ACES

Beginning, origin, primal principle, spark, seed, instigation, primal impetus

Ace of Swords (Seed + rational) = sense.
(Instigation + attack) = act of war.
(Initial + word) = opening address, inaugural talk.
Ace of Batons (Arousal + creativity) = inspirational craft.
(Spark + energy) = anger.
Ace of Cups (Beginning + romance) = first love.
(Start + devotion) = dedication.
(Conceiving + artistic) = designer.
Ace of Deniers (Origin + wisdom) = indigenous lore, an early philosopher.
(Primary + ancestor) = founding father/mother.
(Primal + finance) = capital.

TWOS

Partnership, cooperation, conflict, dialogue, relating meeting, responding, attraction, transaction

2 Swords (Dialogue + mind) = meeting of minds.
(Meeting + aggression) = truce.
2 Batons (Meeting + work) = an office gathering.
(Relating + peers) = work partner.
2 Cups (Cooperation + family) = the family pitch in to help.
(Responding + emotions) = warm reciprocation.
2 Deniers (Conflict + bones) = broken leg.
(Partnership + practical) = methodology for working together.

THREES

Creative growth, expansion, abundance, development,
emerging, manifesting, loss/gain

3 Swords (Growth + struggle) = overcoming difficulties.
   (Emerging + discrimination) = prejudice.
3 Batons (Abundance + work) = plenty to keep you busy.
   (Plan + energy) = power to see things through.
3 Cups   (Expansion + home) = a conservatory or loft conversion.
   (Emerging + sentiment) = budding friendship.
3 Deniers (Loss + money) = lost purse/wallet or cash.
   (Growing + caution) = suspicion.

FOURS

Stability, foundation, rest, order, moderation, rigidity, stagnation

4 Swords (Stability + war) = no end to the conflict.
   (Rest + struggle) = respite.
4 Batons (Stagnant + output) = unchanged productivity.
   (Order + gregariousness) = a staid celebration.
4 Cups   (Stable + feelings) = pacific emotions.
   (Order + yearning) = dissatisfaction.
4 Deniers (Order + possessions) = tidying up.
   (Conserving + finance) = savings.

FIVES

Capability, interaction, uncoordinated, discord, strife, dichotomy,
illness, crisis, challenge, abrasive, division, struggle

5 Swords (Capability + aggression) = soldier, fighter, ready to attack.
   (Abrasive + thoughts) = mental turmoil.
5 Batons (Capability + words) = writer, wordsmith.
   (Uncoordinated + speech) = stammer.
5 Cups   (Illness + romantic) = lovesick.
   (Responsive + crisis) = emergency services.
5 Deniers (Discord + money) = arguing over the bill.
   (Challenge + finances) = bankruptcy.

SIXES

Harmony, balance, health, social networks, community, service

6 Swords (Balance + nerves) = equilibrium after a breakdown.
(Community + discernment) = community survey.

6 Batons (Health + friendship) = making up with a friend.
(Service + sharing) = a charity.

6 Cups (Harmony + pleasure) = a lovely party.
(Network + culture) = museum complex.

6 Deniers (Communal + resources) = an institutional hall.
(Benefit + money) = value for money, a grant.

SEVENS

*Improvement, luck, opportunity, faith, exploring possibilities
action, negotiation, perseverance*

7 Swords (Improvement + justice) = prison reform, recognition of a wrong.
(Negotiation + aggression) = peace talks.

7 Batons (Luck + work) = a great job.
(Perseverance + energy) = ambition.

7 Cups (Opportunity + intimacy) = chance of a hot date.
(Emotional + expansion) = elation.

7 Deniers (Faith + gain) = making an investment.
(Experimenting + finances) = playing the stock market.

EIGHTS

*Accomplishment, consolidation, re-evaluation, change,
refining, direction shift, benchmark*

8 Swords (Refining + thoughts) = making better plans.
(Re-evaluation + belief) = change of religion.

8 Batons (Change + communication) = using another language.
(Enforcing + volatile) = expediency, violence.

8 Cups (Re-evaluation + art) = art critic, redesigning the décor.
(Limiting + intuition) = self-doubt.

8 Deniers (Consolidating + possessions) = making a collection.
(Benchmark + practice) = professional skill.

NINES

Wish, ambition, disappointment, culmination,
rewards, consequences

9 Swords (Ambition + ideas) = a manifesto.
(Culmination + struggle) = suffering.
9 Batons (Disappointment + construction) = slow builders.
(Consequence + impulse) = chaotic results.
9 Cups (Reward + pleasure) = you get the holiday you deserve.
(Increase + devotion) = love's fulfillment.
9 Deniers (Culmination + money) = an endowment policy pays out.
(Disappointment + deeds) = failure to act satisfactorily.

TENS

Success, completion, failure, excess, extremity,
accumulation, dissolution

10 Swords (Success + defence) = you win the chess game.
(Dissolution + reason) = mental decline.
10 Batons (Completion + technology) = the phone is finally connected.
(Extreme + dominating) = tyranny.
10 Cups (Satisfaction + emotion) = happiness.
(Excess + comfort) = feeling smothered.
10 Deniers (Extreme + loss) = catastrophe.
(Accumulation + money) = inheritance.

As you can see, by merely combining each suit's keywords with the number's keywords we arrive at a vast variety of meanings hardly touched upon here. The most work you will be required to do is to learn the characteristics of the four suits and of the ten numbers.

Court cards which combine their rank with the suit keywords are discussed in Chapter 4.

THE CARTOMANTIC PIPS

Here is an alternative, cartomantic version of the pips, which may work better if you like to work from pre-defined meanings. In the cartomantic pips, each number has a significance that helps you to remember the base meaning. As with the suit + number pip method, the combination of the numbers with the suits plays its part, but so does the addition of the baseline of corresponding trumps to help arrive at a meaning. When these are combined, according to the principles here, you can discover further meanings and extrapolations.

In order to fix the suits in your imagination, you can also think of them in a symbolic form as the parts of a tree or representatives of the elements and seasons. You can also embody them as parts of your body.

	TREE	BODY	ELEMENTS	SEASONS	WHEEL
SWORDS	Seeds	Thoughts and words	Air	Winter	I no longer reign
BATONS	Branches	Backbone	Fire	Spring	I will reign
CUPS	Sap/veins	Organs	Water	Summer	I reign
DENIERS	Roots	Hands and feet	Earth	Autumn	I have reigned

The suits can be seen to be emblematic of the Wheel of Fortune with its four positions: the figure rising on the wheel says "I will reign"; at its top, the crowned figure says "I reign"; the person falling from the top says "I have reigned"; and the one below, "I no longer reign" (see opposite).

When the four suits are associated with the Wheel of Fortune, we see that Swords is the least advantageous or most depressive suit in effect, while Cups is the most comfortable. Batons is striving and ambitious, while Deniers tends to rest on its laurels. Together they make a cycle. Further on in Chapter 4, you will find a way of looking at the pips and courts as agents of the Cardinal Virtues, but let us start simply here with some basic correlations.

Another layer of understanding about the pips is possible by associating their numbers with those of the trumps. In this method, the trumps lend their lustre to the pips, coloring their potential. To the playing out of the numbers and suits combined, we can also add pairs of trumps whose numbers echo each pip. So, all the cards numbered five are seen as being resonant with those trumps ending in five: V Pope and XV Devil, which combine the sacred with the profane. The play between these two influences can change the basic pip meanings from a positive, assertive or beneficial reading to a more negative,

The Wheel of Suits,
Minchiate Florentine

I Reign

I Will Reign

I Have Reigned

I No Longer Reign

recessive, blocked or detrimental reading as Pope and Devil play out their saving and destroying qualities. The Fool remains out of this sequence: modern practice has given him zero as his number, but older tarots leave him unnumbered as a tail-end Charlie in tarot sequence.

ASSOCIATIONS BETWEEN PIP AND TRUMP NUMBERS										
Numbers	1	2	3	4	5	6	7	8	9	10
Trumps	I	II	III	IV	V	VI	VII	VIII	IX	X
	XI	XII	XIII	XIV	XV	XVI	XVII	XVIII	XIX	XX
	XXI									

As we can see, three cards are associated with One, but there is only a pair of trumps for the other numbers. Let's look at the major themes arising from these pairs:

Aces Juggler, Fortitude and World: confidence, self-control, completion.
Twos Popess and Hanged Man: relating and trial.
Threes Empress and Death: birth and growth, and death and decay.
Fours Emperor and Temperance: form and balance.
Fives Hierophant and Devil: tradition and salvation, and alternative and damnation.
Sixes Lovers and Tower: choice and consequences.
Sevens Chariot and Stars: triumph and inspiration.
Eights Justice and Moon: truth and mutability.
Nines Hermit and Sun: guidance and illumination.
Tens Wheel of Fortune and Judgement: fortune and resurrection.

These associations may serve as auxiliary reminders in your reading. I've placed them with the cartomantic pip meanings on the pages that follow, so that you have another way of remembering and interpreting them.

I have worked with many different forms of historic cartomancy, from Etteilla's *Petit Etteilla* to early 20th-century cartomancy, and what follows here is recrudescence of that knowledge in a means that is easy to remember. I have retained some traditional meanings from French and Italian cartomancy, such as "a house" for the Ace of Cups or "a journey across water" for 10 Batons: these kinds of meaning have a long history and acceptance among readers. Many of these traditional meanings are also upheld by the small oracles and those that developed out of late 18th-century ways of reading with playing cards, such as the French *Sibyl* cards and the Italian *Vera Sibilla*.

Although it was not the custom to note any reversed cards in historical taromancy, it is true that cards often show their less helpful sides, which is why in the examples below I have assigned definitions under ↑ to signify the cards' customary faces, and ↓ to show their alternative or more severe applications. While you will lay your cards upright, remember that each card has many shades of application and ambiguity. Under each card, I give an example of cards in combination, but please note, *these examples are not the only meanings,* and cards may respond in a variety of ways to any question.

Here is a mnemonic to help you remember the main themes of the cartomantic numbers:

One shows the prime, what's beginning or new,
Strong, sure and subtle, to lead out what's true.
Two brings together a mutual pair;
Gifts and exchanges, and partners who care.
Three is expansion and growing the shoots,
Abundance, dependence and deepening roots.
Four brings authority, order and name;
Door, bed or building, a four-sided frame.
Five's what you grasp with your outstretching hand,
Your struggles and challenges, efforts to stand.
Six for community, together we meld;
Connections, resources, our circle to weld.
Seven for chances and luck that we find;
Touchstones of healing, surprises behind.
Eight for protection for all we achieve;
Changing, adjustments and things to reweave.
Nine for our dreams and our much-wanted wishes,
Extremity, underachievement and misses.
Ten for attainment, completion, success;
Returning and ending, repairing the mess.

ONE

One is governed by the three trumps that have One as their base number:

I Juggler – *Cleverness, trickery*
XI Fortitude – *Perseverance, strength, weakness*
XXI World – *Completion, wholeness, the world turned upside down*

Aces show the basic seeds of our life-shaping primal concerns: health, work, home and finances, as well as what is new or beginning. Aces show us single or independent things where we take the lead or the initiative. Juggler gets us playing with these primal constituents, while Fortitude enables them to grow and be sustained, and World ensures that they are sown everywhere throughout the universe.

Ace of Swords
↑ Health of soul and mind. Power of independent thought. Incisive or cutting-edge ideas. A major decision. A fresh resolve.
↓ Anxiety, fear, indecisiveness, psychically disturbed.
Ace of Swords + 9 Cups = clear vision.

Ace of Batons
↑ Work. Health of the body. Power to create a new enterprise, a new job or post. Signing a document or contract. Male potency. Traditionally, an institutional building – the adjoining card will tell you what kind: e.g. Ace of Batons + 6 Cups = community hall, or Ace of Batons + 10 Batons = office building.
↓ Physical weakness. Work that is difficult to fulfill. A document that needs close attention.

Ace of Cups
↑ House and home. Health of emotions or relations. Power of love and affection. Being comfortable. Female fertility, conception.
↓ Poor relations at home, upheavals at home, a dirty or untidy home.
Ace of Cups + 8 Swords = an upset at home due to something unspoken.

Ace of Deniers
↑ Finances. Health of infrastructure (bones, walls, etc.) Power of resources, seal of approval. A new beginning that lays a firm foundation. Traditionally, a letter, news or a message coming to the client.

Surrounding cards will indicate the nature of the news. Also, a ring or an engagement, a contract.

↓ Check the contract's clauses carefully. A financial scam. A shaky foundation.

Queen of Cups + Ace of Deniers + 9 Deniers = a rich female celebrity of a generous disposition.

TWO

Two is resonant with the trumps that have Two as their base number:

II Popess – *Secrets, wisdom, silence*
XII Hanged Man – *Sacrifice, devotion, feeling stuck, betrayal*

Two represents couples, togetherness and gifts. It flags up dialogues, exchanges and partnerships, which can be mutually compatible or antagonistic. The play between Popess and Hanged Man often provokes issues around staying or departing, being faithful or betraying, being responsible or irresponsible. When a Two is with another Two it often speaks about a pair of something: 2 Batons + 2 Deniers = a pair of earrings or cufflinks.

2 Swords

↑ Separation from the other. Gift of a good idea or suggestion. A dichotomy or paradox. Curiosity. Keeping your own counsel.

↓ Mutual aggravation, incompatibility, retaliation against someone, holding a grudge.

2 Swords + 7 Swords = reconciliation after separation.

2 Batons

↑ Serving together, work colleagues. Gift of work or overtime. A friendly meeting. Traditionally, "a short period of time." Correspondence or news.

↓ Working fruitlessly for someone. Professional jealousy. Exclusion from a social event.

2 Batons + 9 Batons = a short holiday.

2 Cups

↑ Taking pleasure together. A date or evening out together. Dancing. Sex outside marriage. Pregnancy. Gift of love. A mutual exchange.

↓ A secret partnership. A relationship that doesn't progress to mutual satisfaction. An unfaithful partner, jealousy of a partner.

2 Cups + V Pope = marriage ceremony.

2 Deniers

↑ Joint bank account. Business partners or co-sponsors. Gift of money or jewellery. Exchange of money, a personal loan given by you, buying and selling, a bill paid or received. A skill or aptitude by which you earn your living.

↓ Redeeming a loan. Envy. Partners in crime. Minor scam.

2 Deniers + 9 Deniers = an actor.

2 Deniers + 3 Swords = a gift that is lost.

THREE

Three is governed by the following trumps:

III Empress – *Life, abundance, dependence*
XIII Death – *Ending, liberation, unending, stagnation*

Threes govern growth and expansion. What is created from the coming together of Three either enhances all areas of life or can make them problematic. Empress is concerned about growth, while Death sees to the end of all cycles. When ill-aspected, Threes are often in an ongoing but unending state that doesn't find resolution.

3 Swords

↑ Growing distress, illness, loss, exclusion.

↓ Misunderstanding, a worsening situation, interference from another in a partnership.

3 Swords + IV Emperor = loss of authority.

3 Batons

↑ Growing work developments, collaborations. An educational course or top-up training. Fortunate conditions.

↓ Friendships from which you are excluded. Educational progress compromised. Antiquated work procedures.

3 Batons + 10 Swords = suspicions about a collaboration.

3 Cups
↑ Growing family or household. Growth in your environment or home. A young child/toddler. Fertility. An engagement.
↓ A love triangle. Bleeding. Creative plans put on hold.
III Empress + 3 Cups = optimum state of fertility to conceive.

3 Deniers
↑ Growing savings, a small increase in income. Providence for the future. Collecting. Aptitudes and skills you possess. Building. Skills that need further training to enhance them.
↓ Cramped or constrained conditions. Seeking in vain. Remarriage.
3 Deniers + 3 Batons = a pay rise as a result of further training.

FOUR

Fours are under the aegis of these trumps:

IV Emperor – *Authority, order, despotism, inflexibility*
XIV Temperance – *Moderation, balance, unprincipled action*

Fours denote stability, giving us a frame of reference and a place from which to be. Four is traditionally seen as a physical four-sided frame, which is why we see 4 Swords and 4 Cups as a bed, while 4 Batons is a vehicle and 4 Deniers a bank, the meaning according with that of the suit. The rulership of Emperor enables things to take their proper place in an orderly way, while Temperance ensures that they find their own balance and moderation.

4 Swords
↑ Bed of sickness. Confinement in one room or small space, a prison.
↓ Recuperation. Modifying ideas or diet. Caution.
4 Swords + 10 Deniers = a tax rebate or windfall.

4 Batons
↑ Vehicle. Office desk, work area. Computer, electronically generated messages (phone calls, email, etc.) Something is made official.
↓ Vehicle breakdown. Computer malfunction. Bureaucracy.
4 Batons + Ace of Deniers = email or phone call received.

4 Cups
↑ Marriage bed, marital relations, marriage. A partnership is formalized. Anniversary or celebration.
↓ Lack of trust or commitment in the household. Adultery or cheating on a partner.
4 Cups + Page of Batons = sleeping with a co-worker.

4 Deniers
↑ Bank, savings account, deposit box. A rented-out property. A permission, pass or ticket of entry. Honest dealings. Down-to-earth. A stable income.
↓ Materially minded. An enforced change of dwelling. Temporarily homeless. Camping.
4 Deniers + Page of Deniers = a young pragmatist.

FIVE

Five comes under the aegis of the following trumps:

V Pope – *Sacred, salvation, education, bigotry, ignorance*
XV Devil – *Profane, damnation, addictions, temptations, freedom*

Fives reveal our personal domain, the way in which, as humans, we exercise our head and our limbs (think of Leonardo's Vitruvian Man), or how we use our five fingers to grasp and deal with things: efforts, struggles, challenges, as well as motivations, opinions and prejudices play out here. Many of these domains are no longer exclusive to one sex, and each can apply to different individuals and groups. Pope governs what is holy, while Devil deals with the profane: as humans, we strive to find the best way between extremes, doing a little good and a little bad in our lives.

5 Swords
↑ Domain of the mind and spirit. Our attitude to life. Our psychic space. Matters of belief, matters of life and death, code of living.
↓ Religiously bigoted or prejudiced. A surgical operation. Divorce proceedings.
5 Swords + 6 Cups = family shrine.

5 Batons
↑ Domain of work and man, men's matters. Activity or strenuous work, sport, physical exercise. Competitiveness. A "can-do" attitude.

A male relative, boys' rites of passage.

↓ Machismo. Unmanly. Boorishness.

5 Batons + Page of Batons = a sporty young man.

5 Cups

↑ Domain of the home and woman, women's matters. Domestic affairs, things kitsch or cute. Intimacy. The menarche (onset of menstruation). A female relative.

↓ Meddling. Petty gossip. Fickleness. Restlessness in the household. Unwomanly.

5 Cups + 10 Swords = a woman under suspicion.

5 Deniers

↑ Domain of the land, your surroundings or physical space. Ancestral lands. Cultivating a garden or field. The environment. Outdoor equipment.

↓ Loss of property or real estate. Atheist. Untended garden or ground.

Queen of Swords + 5 Deniers = a widow's estate.

SIX

Six is governed by the trumps whose base number is also six:

VI Lovers – *Choice, desire, indecision*

XVI Tower – *Expedience, collapse, avoidance, consequences*

Sixes show us community in action, how we gather together or coordinate, self-govern and make things work in our society through our actions and use of resources. The creation of safe communities. It shows us the nesting boxes or collective networks that create or destroy our whole world, and under whose influence we exist. Doing unto others as we would be done by governs the Sixes. They reveal our connection, trust and sincerity. They also deal with our desires and their consequences. Lovers presents us with the choices that we need to make in order to care best for what we love, while Tower can always destroy speedily what care and community have built.

6 Swords

↑ Aspirations. Ideological community or faith group, finding a new community. A think-tank or spiritual conference. Being proactive as a champion or advocate. A church, temple or place of worship.

↓ Plans that fester. War. Departure or exile from a faith community. A finalized divorce or separation. Revoking ethical mandates. Personal survival.

6 Swords + Page of Swords = the announcement of war.

6 Batons

↑ Passions and enthusiasms. Social or professional groupings, social networks, clubs. Educating the community. Politics, government. Education. Being socially responsible. Male friendships. Professional immunity. A library or university.

↓ Despotic government, a tyrant. Social malaise and unrest. Ignoring friends. Social or personal breakdown.

6 Batons + 6 Swords = a university advocate.

6 Cups

↑ Pleasures. Your immediate circle of friends and family. Family values. Sanctuary of the household, the hearth, what is familiar or accustomed. Local community matters, social services. Female friendships.

↓ Personal passions that injure the web of friendship. Avoiding your nearest and dearest. Caring for yourself.

5 Cups + 6 Cups = women's shelter.

6 of Deniers

↑ Values. International community, welfare and charity in the community. Commonwealth, round-table or United Nations-style discussions. Environmental concerns. Decorating or beautifying your surroundings, or caring for the world at large.

↓ A financial recession, a catastrophe or disaster. Being a cog in the machine. Miserliness.

6 Deniers + Ace of Cups = decorating a house.

SEVEN

Seven is governed by the trumps whose base number is seven:

VII Chariot – *Triumph, gift, movement, lack of direction*
XVII Star – *Hope, inspiration, lost potential*

Sevens denote the way in which we respond to luck or opportunity, and how we act in daily life, for good or ill. Sevens show us touchstones of healing and transformation, if we can use them, bringing us surprises or chances. Sevens also reveal our self-deceptions and dependencies, where things are unraveling, where luck won't support us. Chariot sets things in motion, enabling them to go actively forward, while Star maintains the hope needed to motivate and transform.

7 Swords
↑ Lucky idea. An opportunity to make reparation. Speedy recovery. Dealing with setbacks. An unexpected chance. Self-belief, willpower.
↓ Self-deceit. Frustration, a run of bad luck, plans don't work out.
7 Swords + Chariot = making progress through willpower.

7 Batons
↑ Lucky chance. An opportunity to sort out small irritations, "working through" something, strategizing. A chance to shine in a creative opportunity. Confidence.
↓ Acting defensively. Workaholism. A lost opportunity, losing momentum.
7 Batons + Queen of Batons = a dynamic woman finds a way through.

7 Cups
↑ Lucky break. An opportunity to make peace or reconciliation. A chance to catch up with yourself, a second chance.
↓ Self-indulgence, addiction. Household clutter. An offer you can't refuse.
7 Cups + King of Swords = a drug baron.

7 Deniers
↑ Lucky win. An opportunity to reward or recognize. Self-worth. Winnings or losses from gambling. Sufficient livelihood, publicity (when with a face card), a sense of financial well-being.
↓ Self-doubt. Self-justification. Getting lost in the detail, devalued.
7 Deniers + Ace of Deniers = enough money to buy the ring.

EIGHT

Eight is the base number of the following trumps:

VIII Justice – *Truth, justice, dishonesty, unfairness*
XVIII Moon – *Illusion, dream, miasma, subconscious fears, mutability*

Eights protect what we have and show us how to adapt what we have achieved. Visits, invitations and changes create openings. Eights also question the status quo, testing if we are too safe or need a change, finding what we need to re-evaluate. In a mutable world, nothing is fixed for life, so Eights can herald change, whether from necessity or personal unease, or for the better. Justice enables us to deal fairly and truthfully in our lives, while Moon opens us to other possibilities when doubt and mutability reign.

8 Swords
↑ Health insurance, health check-up. Examining your shortcomings, analyzing your state of mind. Therapy.
↓ Disappointment, ongoing trauma. A one-sided relationship.
A niggling slight, unspoken words or thoughts that smoulder.
Death + 8 Swords = an overdue health check.

8 Batons
↑ Work/labor union, social invitation or working party. Your livelihood or main work. Analyzing your work prospects.
↓ Tired. Feeling trapped in your job. An infection. Malcontent, a strike.
Knight of Batons + 8 Batons = the agent finds you a great job.

8 Cups
↑ Home insurance. Invitation to the home of a relative. Fair play.
An ongoing relationship. Invitation to invest trust in someone.
A protective family member.
↓ Over-protective of loved ones, persecution of family members.
Dissatisfaction with home surroundings.
8 Cups + King of Swords = a family-cases judge.

8 Deniers
↑ Security system. Invitation to share resources. Safekeeping. Incomings and outgoings balance, cash-flow situations, budgeting, numeration or counting.
↓ Unhealthy environment. Unjust settlement, mistakes in your accounts.

8 Deniers + 4 Deniers = a safe.
4 Deniers + 8 Deniers = expenses exceed income.
Knight of Deniers + 8 Deniers = an accountant.

NINE

Nine is the base number shared by:

IX Hermit – *Guidance, isolation*
XIX Sun – *Sociability, success, mania*

Nines deal with wishes, dreams and ambitions. The attainment of certain long-desired things motivates our lives; sometimes we have some partial attainment or we just miss it entirely. Nines are markers for these extremes, which can be very successful or which crash and burn, or where ambition becomes overly grandiloquent. In this mixture of withdrawn and manifest archetypes, Hermit matures over time and solitude through whatever we focus upon, seeking the best guidance, while Sun brings it to light and helps it to flourish, or blasts it with its heat.

9 Swords
↑ Concentrated focus on individual success, someone who achieves best alone. The ability to envisage, psychic skill, visions that sustain you.
↓ Self-harm, mental breakdown. Violent ends, enforced or fated events.
9 Swords + Fool = following the vision in a foolhardy manner.

9 Batons
↑ Traditionally, traveling and holiday; also, exams and tests, graduation, qualifications. Distance and length of time are also indicated, although this may play out as delays. Being in the right place, a travel guide.
↓ Feeling over-exposed. The perpetual student. Settling for second best, setting out in the wrong direction.
Ace of Batons + 9 Batons = passport or travel documents.

9 Cups
↑ Your heart's wish, deepest desire. Gratification. Maturing into happy old age. Generosity of heart.
↓ Your heart's wish comes true but cannot be appreciated owing to circumstances or bad timing. Becoming isolated due to success.

Ace of Cups + Hermit + 9 Cups = a successful retreat center.
Wheel + 9 Cups = being unable to fix upon your heart's wish.

9 Deniers
↑ Someone's wishes for you, also people who are counting on you to respond to their needs. Physical attraction, fame. A bonus or surprise money, maturation of a policy, equity release, services rendered to dependents or others.
↓ Exploitation of your resources, getting burned financially. A miser.
9 Cups + 9 Deniers = celebrity.

TEN

Ten is governed by the trumps whose base number is ten:

X Wheel of Fortune – *Cycle, sequential, unseasonal*
XX Judgement – *Regenerate, return, unredeemed*

Tens denote big things, quantity, accumulation, attainment and completion, as well as what happens when we have an excess of these. Tens border new possibilities and the end or accomplishment of something. They may show the end of a chapter, depending on which cards surround them, as well as the replaying or recapitulation of a major theme in our life. Wheel of Fortune brings everything round in a cycle, both progressively and recessionally, while Judgement recalls whatever is worth revisiting or delivers it to its final destination. The seasons can also be represented by the Tens, in accordance with the trumps' cycles of time.

10 Swords
↑ Obsessions, suspicions, secrets, conspiracy theories. Grief. North, winter.
↓ Paranoia, compulsive behavior. Lies come home to roost. Nightmares. Your worst fears are realized.
10 Swords + World = weltschmertz (world-weariness).

10 Batons
↑ Success in business or work, a lot of work. Traditionally, a journey across water or overseas, or bodies of water in general, from pools to seas. Spring.
↓ Over-ambitious, bearing too many burdens. Déjà vu or a wild goose flying over your grave.
10 Batons + Hanged Man = being a martyr to your work.

10 Cups
↑ Your extended multigenerational family. A successful marriage.
A house extension. A new generation widens the family circle.
A place of entertainment. Summer.
↓ An overwhelming set of household issues. Past infidelities come to light.
The things we do out of love.
7 Deniers + 10 Cups = rewarding the family.

10 Deniers
↑ Financial success or gain, wealth, an inheritance, funds you have saved,
investments pay out, prosperity, ancestral bequest. Playing with everything
to lose. Ancestors and ancestral matters. Autumn.
↓ Tax inspection. Fraud or shady dealings are revealed. Ancestral tendencies
play out in the family. Hoarding. Embezzlement.
Queen of Batons + 10 Deniers = a rich, creative woman.

PAGE

Pages traditionally embody help and support, serving with discretion, able to
perceive needs by being obedient first to wisdom. Each Page is traditionally
seen as a messenger, so look at the card that it is facing to see what that message might be. In a reading, a Page can depict any younger man or woman,
someone who is a student, novice or on trial, or in a supporting role. In terms
of traits, they can depict naive or unformed values, or an unfinished stage of
a project.

Page of Swords
↑ A thoughtful young man or woman. A dexterous and speedy person.
A recruit or someone in uniform. A member of an ethical group.
News that vindicates you. Messages about negotiations.
↓ A gossip. A provoker of agitation or violence. An ex-boyfriend, troublemaker,
a psychotic young person. News detrimental to your reputation.
Page of Swords + 2 Cups = a message about a date.

Page of Batons
↑ An ambitious young man or woman. A friend, co-worker, class- or
teammate. An enthusiast or hobbyist who is always trying new things.
News about surprises or a positive change.

↓ A young zealot. A petulant, spoiled or selfish youth. A faddy dabbler
in new things. News detrimental to your honor.

*Page of Batons + King of Cups = enthusiastic art student visits
a renowned artist.*

Page of Cups

↑ A romantic or gentle young man or woman, a sweetheart or the
Romeo or Juliet on the block. A young blood relative, a bosom friend.
News of a pleasant nature.

↓ A lazy or indecisive young person. An emotionally destructive person,
an aimless youth, a weak and impressionable young person.
News of a disappointment or delay.

Tower + Page of Cups = disastrous news is broken by a simpatico youth.

Page of Deniers

↑ A practical young man or woman. Someone with physical stamina,
can be dogged but always persevering. A student or apprentice.
A professional colleague. A young relative by marriage.
News of your material possessions.

↓ Someone who often loses focus. A vandal, an isolated young person,
a thief. News of a loss.

Pope + Page of Deniers = the priest blesses the young novice.

KNIGHT

Knights are the traditional chivalric embodiment of justice and mercy, defending
the weak, punishing the guilty and maintaining order in the realm. They are go-
betweens with high mobility, so take note of which cards they connect, because
they can reveal a bridging movement: e.g. 10 Batons + Knight of Deniers +
6 Batons = a courier or agent returning from overseas to report to the firm.
Knights often reveal the dynamic at work in a reading. When they appear in a
reading they can depict someone – male or female – with agency, panache,
dynamism or the means to achieve something that the client wants.

Knight of Swords

↑ A champion of causes. A surveyor, a researcher or journalist, a scientist,
a martial artist. A movement that connects with your integrity.

↓ A nasty operator or con artist. An ineffectual Don Quixote with ideas

but no follow-through. A violent or argumentative responder.
A slide into cruel or aggressive behavior.
*5 Swords + Knight of Swords = the operation is performed by
a skilled surgeon.*

Knight of Batons

↑ A creative motivator, an energetic person who gets things done. An ardent
  admirer. A revolutionary or campaigner, an advocate. A movement that
  bridges social divides.

↓ A charming rogue. A fanatic, a jealous or competitive person, an angry
  or hot-tempered person. A slide into impulsive or forceful action.

Knight of Batons + 6 Cups = the lawyer upholds the social care bill.

Knight of Cups

↑ A dreamer. A designer. An attractive person, someone who makes
  overtures of love, a man who invites or gifts you. A movement that
  brings pleasure and peace.

↓ A seducer, a Don Juan or serial adulterer, a pimp, an emotionally
  dishonest fellow. A slide into sentimentality or heartlessness.

5 Batons + Knight of Cups = the sports results are read by a handsome fellow.

Knight of Deniers

↑ A person who is a trustworthy go-between in financial matters: an agent,
  accountant, clerk or courier. A methodical worker. A movement that
  forms a bridge to better order.

↓ A gambler. A grumpy and unsociable man. A workaholic, an imaginative
  number-cruncher. A slide into conservatism or mercenary concerns.

*Knight of Deniers + 8 Cups = the accountant finds mistakes in
your accounting.*

QUEEN

Queens traditionally embody grace and peace, arbitrating and settling the
internal balance of the realm, providing an example of moderation. They are
also trendsetters in their environment who personally embody or exemplify
what best favors their optimum well-being, so see which card the Queen faces
and which one she turns her back upon: e.g. 9 Deniers + Queen of Cups +
Fool, where the Queen is facing 9 Deniers and turning her back on the Fool =

a woman who pursues fame and is unsettled by buffoonery or gaucheness, so this could be an actress who doesn't shine at comedic parts. Queens can be both accessible and demanding, and generally portray adult women who know their own minds.

Queen of Swords
↑ Traditionally a widow or divorcée, an emotionally restrained woman. Control manager, an efficient forewoman or overseer, a discriminating professional, exemplifying the overcoming of struggle.
↓ A woman who stirs things up, a woman who dines out on her misfortunes. A schemer, a sharp-tongued scold, a narrow-minded and opinionated woman, embodying destructive thoughts.
2 Deniers + Queen of Swords = envy is stirred up by the strict woman.

Queen of Batons
↑ A dynamic and creative woman, socialite and hostess. A passionate leader, an optimistic way-shower in troubled times, exemplifying constructive means.
↓ A haughty and domineering person, a drama queen. A rival in love. A woman in burnout, embodying work output.
Queen of Batons + 4 Deniers = a creative woman rents out her home.

Queen of Cups
↑ A trusted friend or confidante. The matriarch of a household. An honest and dependable woman, exemplifying comfort.
↓ An untrustworthy woman, an unfaithful partner. Fickleness. Inability to give comfort, embodying worry.
6 Deniers + Queen of Cups = financial recession affects the generous woman.

Queen of Deniers
↑ A grounded woman with financial acumen and resources. An older woman. A pragmatic stabilizer, exemplifying gain.
↓ An emotional controller. Someone incapable of managing. Someone shored up by affluence or status, embodying loss.
Lovers + Queen of Deniers = the lovers receive a cheque from their grandmother.

KING

Kings traditionally embody royal rule and strong governance. They are patrons of the arts and sciences that build up the city. They have a command and authority that makes them expert, so inspect which card the King faces, as this is the factor that has his attention at present. What lies behind him may be factors that are brewing up that might disrupt his rule: e.g. 6 Deniers + King of Batons + 4 Cups, where the King of Batons faces to the right, shows us that the man is paying exclusive attention to his marriage but is possibly neglecting his responsibility to the community. In a reading, Kings generally portray adult men of experience who are not easily swayed.

King of Swords
↑ A man in authority, a disciplined commander. A widower or divorced
   man. A strategist, an astute judge, an arbitrator, a good regulator ruling
   by maintaining good boundaries.
↓ A hard or uncompromising man, a harsh or humorless person,
   a terrorist leader. Falling into aggression.
King of Swords + Moon = the terrorist sows fear and disquiet.

King of Batons
↑ A dynamic man, a man about town, a vigorous lover. A natural leader,
   a charitable benefactor, a confidant man, ruling with gregariousness.
↓ An egoist, a vain man, a man who exaggerates his own importance.
   An autocrat. Machismo. Falling into impulsiveness.
King of Batons + Ace of Swords = the confident man has a great idea.

King of Cups
↑ A family man. A generous man. An artist, a patron of the arts.
   A humanitarian. An intuitive and compassionate person, ruling with intimacy.
↓ An unfaithful partner. A sentimental man. An ineffectual or whining man.
   A fantasist. Falling into weakness.
King of Cups + 7 Cups = peace negotiator.

King of Deniers
↑ A grounded and steadfast man. A practical provider who likes good
   things. A financier, a merchant, an entrepreneur. An older male relative,
   ruling by good stewardship.
↓ A mercenary or exploitative person, a corrupt financier. A hedonist.

127

An unscrupulous property speculator. A crass or boorish fellow.
Falling into possessiveness.
King of Deniers + Ace of Batons = the entrepreneur signs the contract.

We will explore the court cards further in Chapter 4.

The cartomantic pips require more learning than the suit + number method. They can provide you with a complete system in itself, or act as a basis for a more flexible reading method: it is up to you how you use them.

WORKING WITH THE PIPS

As you have found in this chapter, the pip cards can mean many things, giving endless variations. How do you choose between possible variants of meaning? Skills of reading are given in Chapter 5, but here I offer a few methods to help expand your range of interpretation.

In your reading, always start with a clear question, check the suits and numbers of your cards, and answer the question from the combinations arising in the context of the question. The question can also help to set the agenda for reading the cards. In a question about work, for example, each of the suits might speak about different work aspects in these ways:

Swords show the integrity you use in work, the way you sift or rank priorities, or use your judgement, how you deal with difficulties and discipline.

Batons demonstrate the mode by which you work or cooperate with colleagues, how you trial new methods, how you deal with lack of motivation or multiple demands.

Cups reveal the modulations and changes to work methods, the flow of product to customer, the emotional satisfaction of the workforce, how you recognize blockages.

Deniers show the firm's product and income, its mission statement or promise, its physical location, how you manifest in the market, how you deal with gains and losses.

To this understanding of the suits you could add the values of the pip numbers in order to reveal the nature of a card in a spread about work. Here are a few examples of individual cards:

2 Swords How you assess a colleague; a confrontation about discipline.
5 Batons Adapting to a team; challenging workplace motivation.
7 Cups Varying changes; reimagining the packaging of a product, satisfactory teamwork.
9 Deniers Cumulative production; gross domestic product.

You could create a whole lexicon of work-related meanings for each tarot card, of course, but I hope you can see how fluid this method can be. Set a question of your own and look at the pips with the landscape of your issue as the backdrop: How do the cards speak individually? How do they blend together? For example, a severely ill woman asks, "As my time is short, what is most important for me now?" The pair of cards 10 Batons + 4 Deniers clearly respond with, "Make a will." In the cartomantic method, 10 Batons is "a journey across water," which is often an indication of a departure from the body, not just travel, while 4 Deniers signifies one's income or property: she cannot take it with her.

If working with keywords appeals to you more as a method, then, as you practice, aim to find nouns, verbs, adjectives, objects, actions or qualities for each card. This is a vocabulary that can grow as you become more skilled. The care with which we select words is balanced by the question, which enables us to answer it more precisely.

SUIT INTERACTIONS

Another consideration when reading can be made by the order in which cards arrive. Where one suit comes before another, we may say that it dominates: so Deniers before Batons is not the same as Batons before Deniers. Below are some of the possible blendings or repulsions that can take place. For example, if you have a Denier followed by a Baton you should *read the left-hand column first* for Deniers and then the top line under Batons to find the keywords that reveal the blend (in this instance, ease and comfort).

SUIT	SWORDS	BATONS	CUPS	DENIERS
SWORDS	Struggle, trouble	Ambition, speed	Disruption	Stressed, risky
BATONS	Self-focus	Passionate, convinced	Social, creative	Energy, support
CUPS	Domestic trouble	Love, pleasure	Emotional, intense	Timid, dependent
DENIERS	Poor business	Ease, comfort	Close bonds	Grounded, stable

Here is an example: a businessman asks about what action to take over an intransigent partner who is driving him crazy: 5 Batons, 3 Batons, 4 Cups, 2 Swords, 6 Batons. Without even bothering to read the cards that have fallen on the table, we can see from the suit combinations alone that:

Batons with Batons	This partner is passionately convinced ...
Batons with Cups	... as well as social or creative ...
Cups with Swords	... however, he is trouble ...
Swords with Batons	... because he is terminally narcissistic.

This is what I would call a quick impression, no more, but it does state the situation pretty clearly. This partner is all of these things – talented and very intense – but it is a struggle to deal with him because of his narcissism. The querent knows all this, of course, and his question thus centers on what to do about it.

Reading the cards as they stand, the machismo in their collaboration is beginning to feel pretty much like being yoked in an unequal marriage; separation from the company is the best course. This was a blunt message, and the querent looked dubious at so bald a response, so I asked him to draw out the first trump from the top of the deck, to determine what would happen if the partner remained: the Tower fell out. That much self-focus could result in the collapse of the business, so out goes he! Farewell, partner!

These blendings of suits can give you another tool with which to understand the pips that you have before you. These suit interactions don't always help and are not always required, but use them if you want a quick impression before going deeper.

MULTIPLES

In any spread, we often see multiples of any one number pip arriving. Lots of Eights in a reading might show that someone was at a point of reassessment with their plans, while several Twos would reveal someone beginning to dialogue or coming to a confluence of meeting.

When two pips of the same number show up, note which two suits are present, as well as which two are absent. What kind of suit combination is present in these?

When three pips of the same number arrive together, we always look to see which card of that number hasn't shown up: for example, on page 165 is a reading in which three Fives show up, and the only one missing was 5 Cups.

Since this was a reading about a relationship, it is notable that the suit governing love and the household was absent.

When four pips of the same number arrive, we could have an overwhelming message that this is a mode in which the querent or issue is stuck – a perpetually repeating scenario. In such a case, I would always ask the cards to show me some steps that will help the querent to break the deadlock.

Check the number attributes on pages 112–27 to open up these multiples yet further.

SPREADS WITH THE PIPS

Beginning to work with pips can be challenging if you are stepping out of your illustrated-number-cards comfort zone. The following spreads encourage you to play with the pips and build your confidence.

De Mellet's Pips

This reading is adapted from the Comte de Mellet's 18th-century spread, so that you can practice with your pip cards.

First, remove the twenty-two trumps and set them aside. Then, frame your question.

1   Shuffle together the fifty-six pips and courts. Cut into two equal piles.
2   With pile 1, *with the cards face up,* chant aloud the four suit names: "Swords, Batons, Cups, Deniers" as you deal out one card after the other on a pile: keep any cards that correspond to your chant as you deal them. Go through the pack just once. Keep any matches to one side in the order that they were drawn: these are the suit-drawn cards.
3   With pile 2, in the same way, chant the numbers "Ace, King, Queen, Knight, Page, 10, 9, 8, 7, 6, 5, 4, 3, 2." Keep any cards corresponding to the numbers that you are saying as you deal them out. Repeat twice more, if necessary, until you have between at least one and three cards. These are the number-drawn cards.
    You should now have a few suit-drawn cards, and a minimum of between one and three number-drawn cards.
4   Read the suit-drawn cards *as the story* of the issue in a sequential line.
5   Read the number-drawn cards *as the trigger* or epicenter of the story.
6   To resolve the story, draw between one and three trumps.

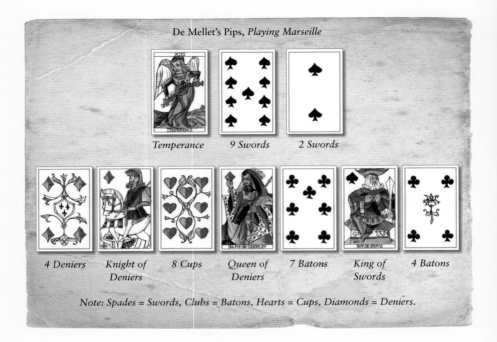

De Mellet's Pips, *Playing Marseille*

Temperance — 9 Swords — 2 Swords

4 Deniers — Knight of Deniers — 8 Cups — Queen of Deniers — 7 Batons — King of Swords — 4 Batons

Note: Spades = Swords, Clubs = Batons, Hearts = Cups, Diamonds = Deniers.

Here, we have a bottom line of suit-drawn cards – 4 Deniers, Knight of Deniers, 8 Cups, Queen of Deniers, 7 Batons, King of Swords and 4 Batons, with 9 and 2 Swords as a pair of number-drawn cards. There are three Deniers, one Cup, two Batons and three Swords, so it is clear that this issue is about financial or mental struggle. The story is about a woman dealing with the estate of her father, together with her brother. It's brought up all kinds of bad associations for her brother that overwhelm him. This legacy of their father should be cause for celebration, but it's not: sorting out the family home efficiently brings sorrow. The burden of it falls upon both siblings, and they are at a standstill. The epicenter of this story, borne out by 9 Swords and 2 Swords, hinges upon the pain and trauma associated with the family house. The decreasing severity of the Swords, from 9 to 2, shows that it is possible to de-escalate the situation. I drew Temperance as a resolution trump: it reminds them that both are still bereaved and grieving, so that a calm sense of proportion will come into play where the work on the estate is fairly shared out.

Three-card Layer

In this spread you read the three trumps and then the pips and courts from their number and suit. You need both trumps and pips in your pack, well shuffled together.

1 Shuffle your question into your pack, then deal each card upright until you come to a trump, keeping any discards that led to this trump and placing them beneath it.
2 Keep dealing until you find the next trump, which starts pile 2, keeping the pips that led to it underneath; do the same for the third trump. You should now have three piles of cards with a trump at the top of each.
3 Read the trumps across as a response to the question.
4 Examine the pip cards beneath the trump in each pile; scan their number and suit. How do these pips and courts support and amplify what the trumps say?

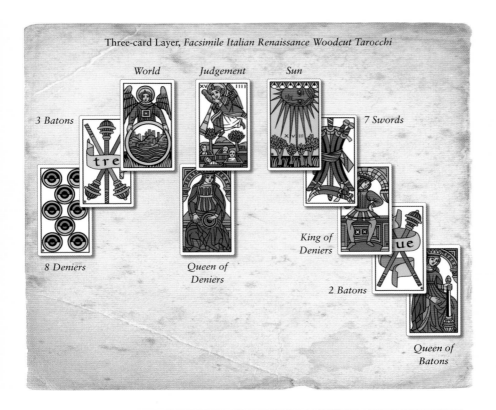

Three-card Layer, *Facsimile Italian Renaissance Woodcut Tarocchi*

World   Judgement   Sun

3 Batons   7 Swords

8 Deniers   Queen of
Deniers   King of
Deniers   2 Batons

Queen of
Batons

In this example, my question is about a PayPal client who was creating trouble for me by demanding a refund but at the same time failing to respond to any of my emails and my attempts to refund him, resulting in his bank taking steps against me. I asked how he might best be satisfied. The three trumps are World, Judgement and Sun: completing this transaction is one thing, but Judgement suggests I've not seen the back of him. I don't want a replay of this situation and am relieved to see the Sun, which tells me that things will resolve successfully. Scanning the pips/courts under each card gives me more information:

8 Deniers and **3 Batons** under the **World**: somehow the money going in and out is stuck in some antiquated system.

Queen of Deniers under **Judgement**: here I am offering the man his money back, but will he take it? I could be dead, for all he cares!

7 Swords, King of Deniers, 2 Batons, Queen of Batons under the **Sun**: trying to make reparation to this retiring man is just fruitless unless I persist with my communication.

The upshot was that this retiring individual was not much of an Internet user and had little idea about checking his email often. I finally went through his bank to leave a message, which was finally accepted by him, and the refund successfully received.

Four Aces Spread

This traditional cartomantic spread sorts out our priorities; it was taught to me by the Welsh cartomancer Jonathan Dee.

1 Remove all four Aces from your pack, shuffle them and lay in positions 1–4 (see top of opposite page) at random. The position and order in which the Aces fall from top to bottom reveals the priorities of your issue:

Ace of Swords	Struggles, ethics, behavior, troubles, thoughts, justification, self-esteem.
Ace of Batons	Work, career, confidence, creativity, skills, gifts, strengths, self-confidence.
Ace of Cups	Emotions, feelings, relationships, intimacy, blending, self-possession.
Ace of Deniers	Manifestation, finance, possessions, practical embodiment, actions, self.

Left	Aces	Right
5	1	9
6	2	10
7	3	11
8	4	12

2 Shuffle the remaining deck and cut into two piles. Use the left-hand pile for cards in positions 5–8, and the right-hand pile for positions 9–12.

3 Read each priority across from left to right as a triplet. I also look at the suit interactions between the outer cards.

4 Cards 5–8 represent the influence, hopes or fears of the querent about the priorities.

5 Cards 9–12 represent the outcome or conclusion of each priority.

This example is for a woman who is going abroad soon for research purposes.

Her top priority is her work: **3 Swords**, *Ace of Batons*, **Sun**
Her enthusiasm for her research is tinged with trepidation, but it is merely travel anxiety.

Next in importance are her relationships: **5 Cups**, *Ace of Cups*, **6 Batons**
She is more used to female company, but this is an opportunity to mix with a professional team. Cups with Batons signifies that this will be a pleasurable experience.

Then come her worries: **9 Swords**, *Ace of Swords*, **8 Swords**
She's really focused on what she wants to achieve, but she should check her innoculations before she travels. Swords with Swords are worries that you need to heed.

Her lowest priority is money: **Page of Deniers**, *Ace of Deniers*, **7 Batons**
Since this is a trip paid for by her sponsors, the woman isn't so worried about the financial side of things. It looks as if she will be assigned a student who will act as a fixer on this research trip. Deniers with Batons presupposes that she will have an easy time of it and that her expenses will be paid for.

Working with the pips represents the steepest learning curve for those who are used to reading with illustrated number cards, or who use set meanings. Do not expect to arrive at a professional grasp of the pips in one attempt: you didn't learn tarot that way the first time, remember! Slowly, patiently and with as much practice as you like to put into it, you will expand your understanding.

Chapter 4

THE CONVERSATIONAL COURTS

Even if the tarot is an ancient game,
It never ages, since it is beautiful:
A game that makes friends, rather than losing them.

But the game of tarot concerns Lords,
Princes, Kings, Barons and Knights;
Which is why it's called the Game of Honors.

VINCENZO IMPERIALI (1582–1648), *Answer to the invective by Lollio,*
translated by Caitlín Matthews

ORIGINS OF THE COURTS

The sixteen tarot court cards, or "honors" as they are known in cartomancy, have not always had queens among them. In the *Mamluk* cards, three male figures are all we find:

TAROT	MAMLUK
King	Malik or King
Knight	Na'ib Malik or Viceroy
Page	Thani Na'ib or Second Viceroy

The three male figures of the *Mamluk* cards still remain in German, Hungarian and Swiss playing cards, where they are called King, Over Jack and Under Jack. But in French-suited playing cards the same figures are known as King, Queen and Valet or Jack. As soon as tarot was developed in Italy, a fourth figure was added to each suit, that of the Knight, with the Italians preferring a King, Queen, Knight and Page for their suits; even in Italian playing cards today, the four courts appear in each suit. The *Cary-Yale Visconti Tarot* sports six ranks of courts: a King and Queen, and a pair of male and female Knights and Pages to support them.[55]

COURTS AND SUITS AS PEOPLE

When it comes to reading the tarot, each suit has a distinctive nature when representing people. In this chapter, we will explore suit and court combinations, as well as find help from the pattern that arises from the four Cardinal Virtues. Here are a few keywords that characterize the courts:

Swords courts Instigating, zealous, ruthless, convinced, direct, exact, argumentative, conceptual, forceful, ethical. Truthful.

Batons courts Vivacious, gregarious, affable, argumentative, flexible, energetic, intentioned, creative, expressive. Strong.

Cups courts Gentle, hesitant, retiring, moody, emotional, intense, compassionate, merciful, interactive. Temperate.

Deniers courts Moderate, precise, cautious, shrewd, secure, enduring, wise, reserved, grounded. Prudent.

These suit keyword characteristics can be combined with the nature of each court title to help create meaning. Again, the keywords below for the court positions are not exhaustive; you will no doubt find and use others:

Kings Commanding, authoritative, stately, unbending, sharing, experienced, prudent, established, releasing, dismissing, completing. An expert or person of power. Kings represent older men or people in authority.

Queens Gracious, accessible, demanding, trendsetters, maturing, mediating, achieving, embodying, receptive, fulfilling. An exemplar or encourager. Queens represent older women and those who set or uphold patterns.

Knights Chivalrous, bold, adventurous, out there, mobile, far-reaching, dynamic, active, manifesting, progressive, focusing, concentrating, independent. An agent or champion. Knights represent fully fledged adults who are active in their field.

Pages Risk-taking, experimental, serviceable, patient, messengers able to liaise, connecting, supporting. A novice or student. Pages represent young people, of either sex, from babies to teenagers.

COURTS BY KEYWORD AND SUIT

The following examples of the combinations of the court keywords and their suit can be seen as a continuation of the list of pips by number and suit on pages 104–7. Remember that this list is not exhaustive, as the combinations in brackets remind you: myriad others await your reading. When courts appear in a reading, they generally represent people who have some of these characteristics.

PAGES

Page of Swords	(Truthful + messenger) = a reliable source.
	(Experimental + ruthless) = a child who tortures animals.
Page of Batons	(Supportive + strong) = a bosom friend.
	(Novice + argumentative) = a student lawyer.
Page of Cups	(Risk-taking + intense) = a teenager without boundaries.
	(Child + moody) = a depressive infant.
Page of Deniers	(Serviceable + reserved) = a shy young waiter.
	(Shrewd + student) = a streetwise student.

KNIGHTS

Knight of Swords	(Zealous + mobile) = a traveling researcher.
	(Progressive + ethical) = a social reformer.
Knight of Batons	(Adventurous + flexible) = an explorer.
	(Affable + independent) = a personable and single man.
Knight of Cups	(Temperate + far-reaching) = a balanced agent of influence.
	(Chivalrous + emotional) = a romantic date.
Knight of Deniers	(Active + enduring) = she/he who leaves no stone unturned.
	(Manifesting + secure) = a good provider.

QUEENS

Queen of Swords	(Demanding + exact) = a martinet.
	(Mediating + concept) = a teacher.
Queen of Batons	(Vivacious + maturing) = a merry widow.
	(Embodying + creative) = an artist or actor.
Queen of Cups	(Compassionate + receptive) = a good listener.
	(Interactive + fulfilling) = a prostitute.
Queen of Deniers	(Cautious + encouraging) = your mother.
	(Gracious + wise) = a *grande dame*.

KINGS

King of Swords	(Commanding + forceful) = a general.
	(Expert + exact) = a top scientist.
King of Batons	(Prudent + expressive) = an official spokesman.
	(Powerful + gregarious) = an influential jet-setter.
King of Cups	(Gentle + releasing) = an anesthetist.
	(Merciful + sharing) = a benefactor.
King of Deniers	(Authoritative + shrewd) = a business CEO.
	(Grounded + unbending) = a convinced pragmatist.

By using only this narrow array of keywords, we can perceive many kinds of personality. For each positive characteristic given here, there will also be their opposites, of course. Someone who is grounded could verge on the unimaginative, just as someone who is compassionate but timid, rather than bold, might become a secret benefactor. It is the context that will help you to gain a sense of the characters who appear in a reading. In Chapter 6, and below, we will also explore how the direction in which the courts face can help our reading.

REMEMBERING THE COURTS

The combinations of suit and rank give sixteen basic personalities around which many different variations dance. A good way of remembering these basic personalities is to equate each of them with a character that you know from fiction or film. My own examples below are taken from Shakespeare's *dramatis personae*; the Pages can also represent Shakespeare's cross-dressing heroines, of course. Make your own helpful associations with figures that are notable in your world.

King of Swords Blood-boltered Macbeth, from *Macbeth*.
Queen of Swords Single-minded Lady Macbeth, from *Macbeth*.
Knight of Swords Deceiving Iago, from *Othello*.
Page of Swords Straight-talking Katherina, from *The Taming of the Shrew*.

King of Batons Convivial party-goer Antony, from *Antony and Cleopatra*.
Queen of Batons The ever-sociable Cleopatra, from *Antony and Cleopatra*.
Knight of Batons Bantering and hasty Petruchio, from *The Taming of the Shrew*, or Hotspur, from *Henry IV*.
Page of Batons Ardent Viola, from *Twelfth Night*.

King of Cups Lovelorn Orsino, Duke of Illyria, from *Twelfth Night*.
Queen of Cups Gracious Olivia, from *Twelfth Night*.
Knight of Cups Romantic Romeo, from *Romeo and Juliet*.
Page of Cups Yearning Juliet, from *Romeo and Juliet*.

King of Deniers Shylock, the moneylender, from *The Merchant of Venice*.
Queen of Deniers Enduring Hermione, from *The Winter's Tale*.
Knight of Deniers Procrastinating Hamlet, from *Hamlet, Prince of Denmark*.
Page of Deniers Faithful Imogen, from *Cymbeline*.

READING THE COURTS DIRECTIONALLY

Here I anticipate Chapter 6, where we look at directional reading. Courts are often the hardest for beginners to read, which is why it is good to set up a significator beforehand, so that you can identify the querent if he or she comes into the reading. (See page 170.) Courts can be people in the client's life – family, partners, children, workmates, friends or employers – and occasionally can be other features or factors. Courts with a pip card can describe a function, action or thought that the indicated person is intending, such as Page of Cups + Ace of Cups = a home-loving boyfriend. Courts with a trump show what kind of dominant dynamic is playing out, as in Devil + Knight of Batons = a young man being ridden by temptation.

The courts in modern tarots often look straight at the reader, but in older tarots the courts only look to left and right, making it possible to read them in a more helpful way. The direction in which the eyes are looking is significant, as we will see in Chapter 6. Courts appearing with other courts are often hardest to read, especially when they clump together, but they can be broken down as follows:

A court facing another court generally expresses interest in it. (a)

Courts facing each other can show friendship and agreement. They are characters in dialogue with one another. (b)

Courts facing away from each other can show disputive or estranged individuals, or characters who are not talking or relating. (c)

Courts of the opposite sex can show marriage or partnership. Courts of the same sex facing each other can indicate a same-sex partnership.

Courts facing each other but with another court next to them or nearby can show a love triangle or an unrequited love with the beloved ignoring them. (d)

Kings face the issues that draw their attention but ignore the issues brewing behind them.

Queens face what will improve their environment but can ignore what they don't want to see.

Knights bridge or convey something from one card by taking it into the card they face.

Pages face the message that they are bringing you. Behind them you may see the sender of the message, or where or why the message originated.

(a) Facing Courts, *CBD Tarot de Marseille*

King of Swords and Knight of Cups   *Page of Batons and Page of Swords*

(b) Courts in Dialogue,
Giacomo Zoni Tarot

(c) Courts Facing Away,
Tarocchi Fine Dalla Torre in Bologna

Page of Batons and Queen of Deniers   *Queen of Deniers and King of Batons*

(d) Love Triangle, *Facsimile Italian Renaissance Woodcut Tarocchi*

Knight of Swords, Queen of Cups, Knight of Deniers

THE CARDINAL VIRTUES IN TAROT

Sitting among the stars, the Imperial sits;
From the heavens descending in a worthy cart,
Beneath a lord, above all others, of kindly heart.

Its wheels are guided by four ladies:
Justice and Temperance with Fortitude,
And Prudence of highest rectitude.

Yoked by a Saracen with wings of gold
Who joins its maker to treasures of old.

DACTALUS DE PADUA, *Imperiale Sedendo – Madrigal in Honor of the Carrara Family*,
translated by Caitlín Matthews

In modern life, virtue is not something we speak much about. We might observe, with G.K. Chesterton, "the act of defending any of the cardinal virtues has today all the exhilaration of a vice" (*The Defendant*). Yet the four Cardinal Virtues still play a strong role in the tarot, revealing a structure that may help us to read with some insight.

The Cardinal Virtues are so-called because they are the hinges (Latin: *cardo/inis*) upon which all life turns. They are first mentioned by Plato in his *Laws*: "Wisdom is the chief and leader: next follows temperance; and from the union of these two with courage springs justice." [56] The Cardinal Virtues are regarded as the basis of an orderly life.

Three of these virtues appear in the tarot under their own names: Justice, Temperance and Fortitude. But what of the fourth? Paul Huson assigns Prudence to the Hermit, following the lead of John Ridrell, who identified Saturn with Prudence. [57] However, following my own teacher Gareth Knight, I have chosen to see Prudence as the World, due to the clues given in the so-called *"Charles VI" Tarot*, also erroneously known as the *Gringonneur Tarot*, which shows the four virtues, each with its own *doxa* or halo. [58] This tarot was made in the early Ferrarese style around 1460–80; these same haloes show up on the Cardinal Virtue cards in the Florentine *Al Leone Minchiate Tarot* of 1790. In the *Minchiate Tarots*, where card numeration is different due to the addition of other cards, giving it forty trumps in all, the Cardinal Virtues of Temperance, Fortitude and Justice come together in the sequence, followed by the Wheel of Fortune. The artist of the *"Charles VI" Tarot* clearly distinguished each virtue,

Cardinal Virtues from the so-called "*Charles VI*" *Tarot*, each denoted by their halo.

Courtesy of Lo Scarabeo

making it evident that they are not human beings but powers; all that remains of their status in the *Tarot de Marseille* are the angelic wings of Temperance, who alone remains non-human in appearance with a star-like flower on her head. Justice and Fortitude have crowns upon their heads, while the World stands naked with unbound hair.

What the "*Charles VI*" *Tarot* also reveals is that each of these figures bears the emblem of one of the suits: the sword of Justice, the broken pillar or column of Fortitude, the cups of Temperance and the orb of the World. If we lay out the suits in tribes, we see that they can be assigned to each of the Virtues, along with the four sets of trumps.

Justice Swords, and the trumps of Hanged Man, Death, Devil and Tower. Justice and the Swords accord with the four trumps that are the agents of integrity and punishment, challenge, temptation and change.

Fortitude Batons, and the trumps of Popess, Empress, Emperor, Pope. Fortitude and the Batons accord with the trumps, who are the executives whose strengths we draw upon in both sacred and secular spheres.

Temperance Cups, and the trumps of Lovers, Chariot, Hermit and Wheel. Temperance and the Cups accord with the agents of our relationship to life, commonly known in the astrology columns of newspapers as "love, progress, health, luck."

World as Prudence Deniers, and the trumps of Star, Moon, Sun and Judgement. The World and the Deniers accord with the trumps that depict the celestial world – the four planetary zones from Earth to the Moon, Sun and stars.

VIRTUE	QUALITIES	EMBLEM	GOVERNS SUIT OF
Prudence (World)	Wisdom, insight	Mirror	Deniers
Justice	Truth, law	Sword	Swords
Temperance	Restraint, modesty	Two Cups	Cups
Fortitude	Strength, courage	Pillar	Batons

The Cardinal Virtues of the classical world thus appear in most historical tarots. In the ninety-seven card *Minchiate*-style tarot decks, which appeared from the 16th century onwards, the Cardinal Virtues were further supplemented by the addition of three Theological Virtues from the letters of St Paul: Faith, Hope and Charity.

The co-relationship of the Cardinal Virtue tribes, seen in the diagram below, gives us the opportunity to meditate on the shape of the tarot trumps and their four fields of influence, showing that not only are the suits related to each

	STAR	MOON	SUN	JUDGEMENT	
WHEEL		**PRUDENCE** (WORLD)			HANGED MAN
HERMIT					DEATH
	TEMPERANCE	JUGGLER		**JUSTICE**	
CHARIOT					DEVIL
		FORTITUDE			
LOVERS					TOWER
	POPESS	EMPRESS	EMPEROR	POPE	

The Cardinal Virtue Families

other – with Deniers opposite Batons, and Cups opposite Swords – but they are also related to the trumps. This division of the tarot into tribes leaves out the trump of the Fool, which historically enjoys a lower status than the other trumps, with the Juggler as the pivot of this pinwheel of fortunes.[59] On his table lie the four suit emblems: below, the archetypal wielders of those emblems are shown in macrocosmic style (see diagram opposite).

THE COURTS AND THE CARDINAL VIRTUES

We can deepen our understanding of the courts by observing how each rank is also associated with one of the Cardinal Virtues:

Justice corresponds to the *Knights*
Knights are the embodiment of justice and mercy, defending the weak, punishing the guilty and maintaining order in the realm.

Fortitude corresponds to the *Kings*
Kings embody royal rule and strong governance, patrons of the arts and the sciences that build up the city.

Temperance corresponds to the *Queens*
Queens embody grace and peace, arbitrating and settling the internal balance of the realm, providing an example of moderation.

Prudence/World corresponds to the *Pages*
Pages embody help and support, serving with discretion and able to perceive needs by being obedient first to wisdom.

Thus, we can see each of the ranked courts as agents of the Cardinal Virtues, which may further help to determine what function they are playing in a reading and providing prompts for reading. The age in which we live usually discounts the Cardinal Virtues: while Strength is lauded for its forthright action, Justice is often disputed or absent and at the basis of much unrest, Prudence is hardly valued, and Temperance has become the least of all the virtues in an age where excess rules. Since many problems arise from the imbalance in the virtues in our world, they reflect strongly in our readings; we can look to the courts – the actors in the stories we are attempting to read – as wielding particular power to harmonize, or to express indulgence or deficiency, in those stories.

In his *Nichomachean Ethics,* [60] Aristotle spoke of the virtuous habit of action as being the intermediate state between opposing vices, or excess and deficiency, whereby either too little or too much is inadvisable. If we follow Aristotle, we can see how these virtues might be attributed to the four suits of the sixteen court cards. In the table below I have assigned one of the median virtues, along with its deficiencies and excesses, to each of the courts, giving you another possible way of understanding how they might be read.

We can immediately see how these virtues might help you read the courts as they arise, both in respect of these Aristotlean virtues and as agents of the Cardinal Virtues themselves.

COURT	DEFICIENCY	VIRTUE	EXCESS
The Suit of Swords			
KING	Corruption	Integrity	Legalism
QUEEN	Foolishness	Discrimination	Judgementalism
KNIGHT	Envy	Righteous indignation	Malicious enjoyment
PAGE	Understatement	Truth	Boastfulness
The Suit of Batons			
KING	Cowardice	Courage	Rashness
QUEEN	Meanness	Generosity	Prodigality
KNIGHT	Cantankerousness	Friendliness	Obsequiousness
PAGE	Sloth	Diligence	Workaholic
The Suit of Cups			
KING	Meanness	Magnanimity	Indulgence
QUEEN	Selfishness	Love	Enablement
KNIGHT	Licentiousness	Temperance	Strictness
PAGE	Shyness	Modesty	Shamelessness
The Suit of Deniers			
KING	Disregard	Respect	Idolatry
QUEEN	Pride	Humility	Degradation
KNIGHT	Impatience	Patience	Irascibility
PAGE	Boorishness	Wit	Buffoonery

Where Two Courts Meet

Here is a spread that I invented for the New York Reader's Studio in 2011. It doesn't involve reading more than six cards, even though it looks very impressive when laid out. It uses all of your court cards. In fact, you will also need another tarot deck. Yes, that's *two* tarot packs. Decide which deck is your reading deck; from the second tarot you will need only the court cards, which are used to frame the tableau. If you have only one deck, then cut pieces of paper *of the same size* as your tarot and label each one to represent all sixteen courts. This spread needs a clear table, floor or bed to lay out the cards because it's a big one.

Use this spread when the issue concerns the nature of the contract between two people who are in a relationship as lovers, partners, boss and employee, room-mates, etc. The ethics about asking questions concerning someone other than the querent is something we should take seriously: to ask about someone else is like psychic surveillance, and we have far too much of that already in the world! But this method may illuminate how the interaction works out.

1 Randomly lay out sixteen court cards *from another tarot* in a square: four cards on each side, leaving an indentation at each corner so that, within the square, there is room to lay at least sixteen piles of cards inside it. The order doesn't matter. It should look like this, with a space at each corner, with the sixteen courts forming the basis of a grid:

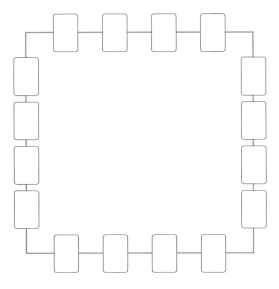

2 The querent now chooses *two* significators from the rows of courts to represent each party in the issue, one for her/himself and one for the other party. *Ensure that one significator is on a horizontal line and the other is on a vertical line.* Move them to a different position if necessary.

3 The querent now shuffles the complete reading pack and the reader deals out *the whole pack* face down into the sixteen positions within the square, four cards per pile, creating a series of sixteen piles of cards within the frame. There will be fourteen cards left over: this is the Ally Pack. Set this aside.

4 Now, just as you consult map references, check which is the square that marks the point where the two significators would meet if they both stepped forward into the frame. Use that single pile of four cards only. The Grid of Sixteen should look like this: here, C = a court card. I've included arrows to show where the two chosen courts meet at Pile 6: this is the pile of four cards used here.

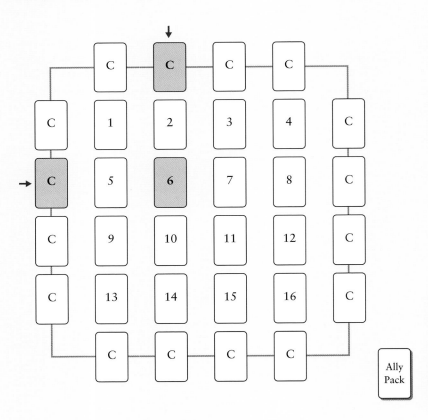

5 The four cards (in this case in Pile 6) that arise from the meeting between the two edge significators, when read in order, show:

- ◉ The understanding/disagreement between the two.
- ◉ What can work out between them.
- ◉ What has to be negotiated between them.
- ◉ What is still to be uncovered/revealed between them.

6 You can also draw one or more card at random for each individual from the Ally Pack to amplify or clarify the reading.

In this example, an artist is looking at her collaboration with an author whose work she has been assigned to illustrate by the publisher. Knowing nothing about the author, the artist sets up her tableau, choosing to represent herself as the Queen of Batons and the author as the King of Deniers. The four cards that come out of the meeting square are:

3 Cups She is relieved that they can make a good working team with a bit of give and take.

Temperance The flow of ideas can be negotiated amicably.

9 Deniers The author has a firm idea of what he wants and is likely to be demanding. She adds from the Ally Pack to clarify. Tower and 4 Batons: there may be a meltdown before they reach a point of stability, attainable by an exchange of emails.

9 Swords This author is used to working alone. From the Ally Pack, the artist adds Sun and 2 Cups: having goodwill helps with any rapprochement arising from this.

Now that you have all the skills to read trumps, pips and courts, it is time to get to work.

CHAPTER 5

Divining Skills from Earlier Eras

❦

The fact that card meaning changes in each reading does not mean
we should not trust the messages we see in it. Everything is a sign.

YOAV BEN-DOV, *Tarot: The Open Reading*

THE QUESTION: NARROWING THE APERTURE

Divination is not a random action but a purposeful one, whereby we frame a question in order to discover the answer. The more exact the question, the more efficient the results, as you can see from any Web search: if you simply type "cars" into a search engine, the possibilities are countless, but if you refine your search to "Classic BMWs 1960–62," you are presented with more exact results. The action of asking a precise question narrows the field of enquiry, creating an aperture which focuses more closely upon the issue. The vaguer the question, the vaguer the answer.

First determine your criteria: let's say the issue is about moving house. By itself that is not a question, simply a concern that is weighing on you.

What is it you want to know or learn? (e.g. about the coming move.)
What guidance are you seeking? (e.g. how will the move go? What do
I need to be aware of in this move?)
What are the specifics of the question? (e.g. you are worried about the
effect of the move upon your child.)

Now, the question about the move can be more exactly framed as:

(General enquiry) "How will the coming move go?" *or*
(Guidance about an action) "What do I need to be specifically aware of
in this move?" *or*
(Specific information) "What will be the effect of this move upon my child?"

These are three different questions, giving very different results. Some questions do not give helpful advice, and these are best avoided:

- Yes/no questions yield little information and confuse the oracle.
- Either/or questions: read for one option, then read for its alternative.
- Questions involving another person turn your cards into an unethical surveillance device. Ask advice for yourself rather than *about* someone else.

Historical bad question-framing from the 4th century BC reminds us to be careful. King Croesus of Lydia asked the Delphic Oracle, "Should I go to war against the Persians?" (a yes/no question). The response came, "If Croesus goes to war he will destroy a great empire."[61] As was subsequently borne out, Croesus wrought the destruction of his *own* empire because he did not understand which way the oracle was answering yes/no: Had he asked "What are the consequences of going to war with Persia?" he might have been more cautious. Ambiguous questions bring ambiguous answers.

Useful question formats include:

- Give me guidance on ....
- Show me the consequences of ... (a plan, trip, decision).
- Show me how to move forward from ... (the current situation).

Understanding the answer to your question is another matter, of course:

- Cards may tell you something you already know or suspect, giving you a second opinion or confirmation.
- Answers may arrive in a metaphorical or symbolic way, as in dreams. Always relate the answer back to your question.
- If the answer is unclear, look again at your question and refine it more precisely.
- The cards give you a snapshot of *things as they are at this moment*. Any action you take, any decision you change, will alter things. Cards are not the instruments of immovable fate.

It is always good to read the cards from the standpoint of the present moment. The question may be about the future, but the roots of the future lie in what we can discern from the aperture that the question has made, where the issue is framed by the present circumstances. Consider the advice of any answer and try it: nothing is fated, and the decisions we take as a result of information received from a reading will make changes, which will in turn change the future.

BASIC SKILLS

The following basic skills may be obvious to the experienced taromancer, but I provide them here for both the beginner and anyone learning to read with historic tarots for the first time.

Mixing, Shuffling and Re-ordering the Cards

Some folk can shuffle, some cannot. If you are one of the latter, lay the pack face down on a clean surface and spread it out in a line, pulling out cards randomly. The results will be just as good! Some older tarots don't come with the rounded corners of modern cards and can be uncomfortable to shuffle, while others are very large indeed. Some people like to shuffle their cards by mixing them on a table, swirling them round and round; this results in many reversed cards, which we are not reading here.

Occasionally, individual cards keep returning to your spreads, however well you shuffle. When this happens, shuffle the card into your tarot, asking what it is trying to show you. Turn the tarot face up, looking through it until you find where the card has fallen, and read the pair of cards on either side of it. However, if you keep getting the same cards from a previous shuffle because the card is behaving like a marked card in a conjurer's deck, then the cards probably need to be re-ordered. Deal out the whole pack into eight piles, one card at a time, pick up the piles at random, and start working again.

Turning the Cards Face Up

One of the skills we use in cartomantic tarot reading is holding the pack face up in order to look through and see where a particular card has fallen. For many taromancers, this feels radically wrong, as we are used to pulling out cards randomly with their backs towards us, but this method is required in a few spreads and always arises out of a prior randomization of the cards.

If you have a specific issue that one card will represent, whether it is a chosen significator or just a topic card, such as Ace of Cups to signify your house in a house sale, you can shuffle and mix, turn the pack up and see where this card has fallen: each one of the brief examples in the trumps and pips sections in Chapter 3 was chosen like this. Check the cards that cluster about the card or the pair of cards on either side of it. This method reveals what you want to know just as well as laying out the cards from the top of a shuffled deck, and can be a useful method when you are on the move and unable to lay down cards on a surface.

When searching through a tarot for one or more cards, it is helpful to consider the whole pack *as a continuous book of pages,* as if it were turning like a revolving door on a central pivot. This way, if the card you seek falls at the bottom of a face-up pack and you are required to find the cards that support it on either side, then that bottom card is thought of as being contiguous and sequential to the top card in your hand.

Increasing and Decreasing

Cards with the same suit that lie together in a line can increase or decrease in their numerical value. For instance, 3 Deniers followed by 4 Deniers is showing that the money is growing; 4 Deniers followed by 2 Deniers shows that the money is scarcer. When someone is unwell, the reduction of their condition signals a return to health, as we would find in a question about recovery that throws up 8 Swords followed by 3 Swords: the severity of the illness is declining.

Color

Some taromancers also like to divine from the color predominance of cards: e.g. red = energy, life; blue = heavenly, mental, and so on. But since deck coloration is so very variable, I have never personally found this method very helpful, except when you get a coagulation of one color together, as when Temperance, Popess and Justice fall together and a large amount of blue floods the reading. The earlier historic tarots do not have more than three to five colors in them, due to the block-printing process whereby each color had to be separately applied to the resultant print (hence why their palette is so restricted), so this method is rarely useful save in modern recolored reproduction tarots. These are merely suggestions for reading:

Black   Heavy, manifest reality
Yellow Light, illumination, golden, sun
Red   Dynamism, passion, energy, blood
Blue   Reflection, restraint, calm, sky, sea
Green   Nature, growth, earth
White   Lightness, disembodied, spiritual reality

Modern printings of historical tarots often employ a much wider set of colors, including purple, light and dark blue, mulberry reds and browns, while flesh color is mostly the same as the card background in older decks.

Ambivalent Cards and Reversals

Before the late 18th century, tarots were read upright. It is only in the modern books about the *Tarot de Marseille* that we find reversals. This is a recent development, of course, designed to cater for those whose reading vocabulary now includes reversals. It originated with Etteilla, who used reversals to enable a wider vocabulary in his *Petit Etteilla,* using only thirty-two playing cards (four suits of just the Ace, King, Queen, Jack, Ten, Nine, Eight and Seven). By so doing, he gained sixty-four upright and reversed meanings, as well as further sideways combinations.[62] Following his lead from *Petit Etteilla* and from his tarot pack *Book of Thoth,* taromancers have used reversals ever since. Of course, handling cards often results in their becoming reversed. While we have little information about how reversals were dealt with, in this book I am using and depicting all cards as upright, although my interpretation will sometimes reveal their darker or alternative sides.

Regardless of whether you note and use reversals or not, you will often find that cards show a certain ambivalence when you read them, even if they are upright. Not only can they be read in many ways, but even within the margins of the question posed they can reveal different shades of themselves. This very ambivalence is challenged when a card is combined together with others. A jolly Sun can turn out much less sunny when sandwiched between the Page of Swords and 10 Swords, for example, especially when the question is, "How will his actions affect me?" Such a combination of cards with that question might say, "The young troublemaker will expose you in the worst possible way." So we have to be flexible.

For example, you have a major project coming up and ask about an aberrant colleague, "How far can I rely upon him to support me?" You draw the Knight of Swords, Judgement, the Ace of Batons: superficially, the cards seem to say, "The man is returning to his initial work." However, the only male card, the Knight of Swords, is facing away from the other two cards. You've given this man many second chances and he is still not facing the issue for which you need his support. By laying another card to see what he is facing, 3 Deniers, it becomes clear that he is more interested in the financial returns and not in your project at all. Here, you cannot read the Knight of Swords as your champion in any regard: he's a man more interested in tilting at financially promising windmills.

The context alone tells us that the Knight of Swords isn't read in its most affirmative aspect, so you now conclude that this spread is saying, "The man is returning to his initial obsession."

Is He Reliable? *Vergnano Tarot*

| 3 Deniers | Knight of Swords | Judgement | Ace of Batons |

Checking the Bottom Card

Drawing a bottom card from the pack after you have laid the cards is a revealing technique. It can show you the unseen help or potential that the client can draw upon, or reveal something unknown. The taromancer Rachel Pollack calls it "the teacher card." I frequently draw it out to understand a hidden motivation or worry. In a question about surviving the winter while unemployed, the bottom card of 5 Deniers is probably talking about some small savings salted away or debts that could be called in.

The bottom card can also flag up a warning, so if you drew Hanged Man in a question about the speedy completion of a house sale there might be something treacherous that hasn't been noticed: it would be best to check the paperwork with your lawyer.

The bottom card might also reveal hidden motivations or attitudes. For example, when someone asks about going on a family holiday and the bottom card is Hermit, it is time to wonder how much the querent wants to go, because it looks as if he or she would rather be alone.

BLENDING CARDS

One card by itself has a neutral value, but as soon as you lay one card beside another, the two blend together like two shades of wet watercolors, making a third color. So let's now look at some examples of how two cards can blend together (see overleaf).

Blending Cards (i), *Vandenborre Tarot*

Death

9 Deniers

By itself, each card has its own neutral value.

Death Stripped back to essentials, cancellations or endings.
9 Deniers (Culmination + money) = savings.

However, when we ask a question, suddenly we have a new dynamic activating those neutral cards into specific meaning. Now, if a woman asks what her newly married daughter would like as a gift and she draws the cards above, we know that Death is about endings, and that 9 Deniers is about an accumulation of money. In this context, we can understand that the querent is being advised to liquidate an insurance or savings policy, to help her daughter start her married life with a large sum of money.

Blending Cards (ii), *Vandenborre Tarot*

9 Deniers

Death

But what if a man asks about how his investment will fare during a time of troubled economy and he draws the same two cards, but as 9 Deniers + Death (see Blending cards ii)? The answer is that his savings get wiped out. Death in the *Vandenborre Tarot* faces left, so he turns his scythe towards the heap of Deniers. So we see how the same two cards can give very different meanings because of the question and their sequence. In the woman's gift, Death came first, followed by 9 Deniers, saying "End the savings!" But in the man's investments, 9 Deniers came first, followed by Death: visually, you can see how Death literally reaps the Deniers, and how the cards say, "The investment is wiped out."

Let's say you receive an excited but garbled phone message from a friend but can't gather the gist before she is cut off, so you ask the tarot, "What news is she bringing me?"

Here, the cards give us 7 Batons (energetic + perseverance) and 9 Batons (ambition + desire); see below. You note that the cards are from the same suit and that they are rising in number: two Batons tell us that the news most likely concerns work, and that something about work is greatly extended or increased. As you blend the two cards together, you read, "Her pursuit of promotion is rewarded with a more responsible post" or, "Your friend's promotion wish is fulfilled."

Building the story from the way the cards blend together begins with any assemblage of cards, whether it be just two or twenty-two. Practice pairing cards by cutting your tarot into two piles and turning up one card from either pile at the same time, reading and blending what is drawn. To sharpen your practice, combine this with a series of brief questions to help reveal what the pairs are saying.

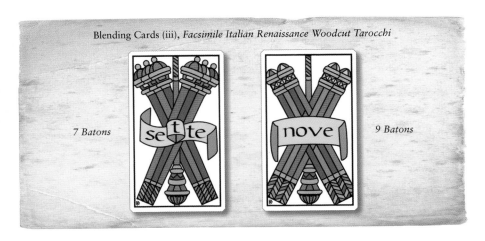

Blending Cards (iii), *Facsimile Italian Renaissance Woodcut Tarocchi*

7 Batons

9 Batons

READING IN LINES

If we want to read authentically and historically, we don't always have to lay our cards in fixed positions; we can just read the sequence of the story in the cards. A line of cards, laid left to right, can be read like a storyboard or cartoon strip; with the sequential unfolding of the story, each card becomes a land feature in the querent's landscape, and you, as the taromancer, read the lie of the land. Lay as many or few cards as you like, but the story will certainly have a fixed term to it. Most lines are laid in odd numbers of three, five, seven or nine cards, giving you a central hinge card.

There are several methods of reading a line, including:

- Reading the cards in straight sequence.
- Mirroring cards by relating the opposite ends of the line together.
- Associating certain clumps of cards with one another.

Here, an applicant for a university post asks, "On what basis are they hiring at the university for this post?" She's been caught out before by being unprepared for the hirer's particular expectations. The cards are 4 Deniers, 2 Cups and 6 Swords. Here I'll use the cartomantic pips method, spelling out how we arrived at the conclusion.

Line-reading, *CBD Tarot de Marseille*

| 4 Deniers | 2 Cups | 6 Swords |

4 Deniers Four resonates with both Emperor and Temperance, so there's a sense of authority and moderation at work. When we add the suit concepts of Deniers (practical, grounded, secure), we get the sense that the university wants someone who is able and stable; also that this post may come with tenure.

2 Cups Twos resonate with Popess and Hanged Man, so a mixture of learning and staying power mixed with the suit of Cups (responsive, devoted, intuitive) gives us a sense of the university wanting someone who can apply themselves to research in an independent way but who is also able to be reciprocal and responsive.

6 Swords Sixes relate to Lovers and Tower, or choices and consequences, and when mixed with the Swords (rational, verbal, ambitious, intellect) we see the university wants a strong-minded person who can discern clearly and still work in a team.

The applicant now has a better idea of which qualities to flag up in the interview: she needs to show how modestly hardworking she is, how she can work alone but also in a team, that she is someone who has done independent research and whose discerning intellect will be an ornament to this university. We also note in these cards that both 4 Cups and 2 Cups have a shield upon them, giving us a sense that this university is proud of its traditions and has a reputation to protect.

We can also unlock a line of cards by taking the bottom card of the shuffled deck as the key card that reveals the issue and reading the line as an unfolding story in relation to it. This example comes from a class where I was using historical questions to better flag up how the cards reveal things. Retrospective questions about history are a great way of boosting the confidence of beginners, I find: what one of my students calls "divining in retrospect"! Here I asked, "What was Sir Thomas More facing at the time of his trial in May 1535?" (See illustration overleaf.)

Using cartomantic pips, the key card shows us that the issue is about divorce proceedings, while the sequence tells us that a steadfast man (Sir Thomas More) and a hard man (Henry VIII) each have their own vision, on which neither will compromise. Both Kings are facing right here, looking at 9 Swords, which is a card showing someone going it alone, no matter the odds; it can also be read as the card of self-harm or even martyrdom. As we know, Henry wanted to divorce his first wife, Katherine of Aragon, and force everyone to acknowledge Anne Boleyn, the woman who would become his second.

Unlocking the Line, *Tarot de Marseille Pierre Madenié 1709*

Key card

5 Swords

King of Deniers   *King of Swords*   *9 Swords*

On this point, Thomas More's refusal to compromise Church teachings led him to the scaffold, and Henry sentenced his friend to execution; Thomas was canonized in 1935 as a martyr.

DIRECTION OF READING

How do we know in which direction to read the cards? In the era before universal literacy, the direction of card reading was often from right to left; early cartomancers, like Etteilla, certainly read that way.[63] In the 21st century, taromancers tend to read from left to right, just as we read most languages using the Roman font.

Left-to-right reading has created certain conventions in taromancy that we need to consider: in terms of sequence, is the card on the left before or after the card on the right? Does the left-hand card have a primacy over the one beside it? Etteilla spoke of cards in his right-to-left reading as "falling upon" the next left-hand card, so that the first card in the sequence was considered to be more powerful and have influence upon the one that followed it. These considerations become important when we blend cards together. Sometimes other factors need to be considered, too.

If I lay the Queen of Cups and place 8 Swords next to it, and then Wheel of Fortune last, is the Queen of Cups causing a response in 8 Swords that leads to another event, or is it simply the condition she is in or the action she takes next that causes the wheel to turn? This could become an issue of subject or object, as the following phrases demonstrate, telling different stories:

QUEEN CUPS	8 SWORDS	WHEEL OF FORTUNE
The generous woman ...	reconsiders ...	the timing, or
A housewife ...	accomplishes a coup ...	at the tombola, or
The barmaid ...	de-escalates aggression ...	over the pub quiz.

In each of these alternative readings, the subject is the Queen of Cups, 8 Swords is the verb or action she takes, while Wheel of Fortune is the object of the sentence. If we re-order the cards:

8 SWORDS	WHEEL OF FORTUNE	QUEEN OF CUPS
Disappointment ...	has turned ...	her unfaithful.

WHEEL OF FORTUNE	QUEEN OF CUPS	8 SWORDS
The passage of time ...	makes the woman ...	reconsider her health.

Now the Wheel of Fortune, being a trump, may have a bigger influence over a pip card in your mind, or the Queen may indicate the querent and be important in its own right, or the 8 Swords could be a decisive circumstance that is leading the story. The way in which you speak the story aloud from the cards before you is determined both by the order of the cards and also, of course, by the manner and syntax of your language.

Ultimately, as we saw earlier with Death and 9 Deniers (see page 156), the way we read and blend cards is usually led by the question itself, whereby the sequence of storytelling is clarified. However, as we shall see in the directional reading method, sometimes the story can hop about. (See also Chapter 6.) Experiment by laying cards and speaking aloud the story. Whichever way you choose to read, bear in mind that the sequence – in terms of storytelling or timing – and dominance of one card over another will be led mostly by the question, which enables the story to be told.

The Line of Cardea and Janus

This method shows how a line can be read through a sequence of processes, each of which cumulatively reveals meaning: this is where the story can jump about a bit. The central hinge card is named for Cardea, who was the Roman goddess of the Door Hinge, with her festival at the kalends of June. She is related to Janus, the god of the Year's Door, in January, who looks backwards and forwards simultaneously; here, he governs the mirroring in this line.

1 In a line of five cards, read the center card as the hinge or pivot: this is Cardea's card.
2 Read the three middle cards as showing the heart of the matter.
3 Read the first three cards as the outset of the issue.
4 Read the last three cards as the conclusion, with the final card as an outcome.
5 Read card 1 with card 5, card 2 with card 4. These are the Janus cards that mirror each other. They can reveal a hidden dynamic.
6 Read cards 1, 3 and 5 as a summary.

Usually, a line reveals itself pretty easily and you don't need to do the whole sequence, but in the example that follows I go through all the processes, so that you can see for yourself how to read without positional meanings. This question was for a harassed querent who phoned me to ask, "What is going on with my television and how can it be fixed?" Here, I am using the number and suit method of reading.

Line of Cardea and Janus, *Tarocchi Fine Dalla Torre in Bologna*

| 9 Swords | Knight of Swords | 3 Swords | Juggler | Ace of Deniers |

9 Swords Communication + engagement
Knight of Swords Zealous + technical
3 Swords Growing, struggle
Juggler Skill, clever
Ace of Deniers Starter + money

The entire line reads, "The woman's television needs an engineer with a greater experience to solve the matter. Unfortunately, it requires an outlay of money." Three lots of Swords tells us that things are problematic and I will be delivering bad news. The hinge of 3 Swords is why the querent has phoned me: she's technically struggling. The Knight of Swords, 3 Swords and Juggler tell us that we need an expert on the scene. The combination of 9 Swords with Knight of Swords and 3 Swords tells us that TV transmission has been cut off and she has lost vision. The 3 Swords, Juggler and the Ace of Deniers say that, for this loss, a skilled engineer is needed and it is going to cost. Mirroring the cards: 9 Swords with the Ace of Deniers says that a TV with actual transmission will involve the outlay of money. The Knight of Swords with Juggler says the engineer is an expert. As it turned out, the TV was utterly broken and needed replacing, hence the capital outlay of the Ace of Deniers. Also, the electrical wiring in the house needed fixing, which is visually suggested by 9 Swords, but I missed this detail.

Cross and Passport

Based on the classic French Cross, here the Cross (cards 1–5) shows the situation itself, while the Passport (cards 6–8) reveals the way cards 1–3 can move on. It mixes positional meanings with a cartomantic line. Using your whole deck, lay out the cards like this:

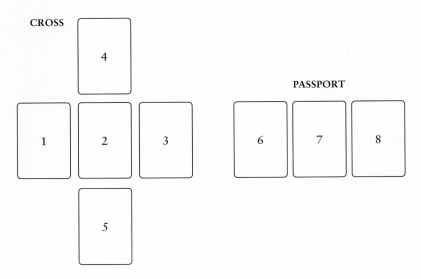

Card 1 The querent's situation.
Card 2 The issue itself.
Card 3 What the querent is facing.
Card 4 Advice or what to do.
Card 5 Outcome or what not to do.
Cards 6–8 These are read as a line, then as amplifications of cards 1–3: mirror 1 + 8, 2 + 7, 3 + 6, reading them together.

If you want to practice your pips, then lay only majors on cards 1–3 and only pips on cards 6–8 by taking the first majors or pips to come out of a turnover.

People very often want things that are detrimental for them, as in this case, where I used the Cross and Passport. The young woman asked a commonly posed question: "How can I get my boyfriend back?" I finally allowed this question only because she could not see past it. But, as you'll see, the cards answered her very exactly about the consequences of her wish.

The Cross

Judgement = the querent. Judgement is a classic card of return, so she will get her wish. However, during our session, I understand that this situation of her boyfriend leaving and returning has arisen more than once, and that he has not treated her well.

Fool = what she is facing. This is the tarot speaking very truthfully – she has a vagabond, ne'er-do-well boyfriend.

5 Deniers = how she can deal with it or what she can do. She can continue to struggle with her finances if he does indeed return.

Hanged Man = the outcome or what not to do. She will end up dancing attendance upon him, or she can choose not to go down this route.

5 Batons = the issue itself. How much of a passionate struggle does she really want?

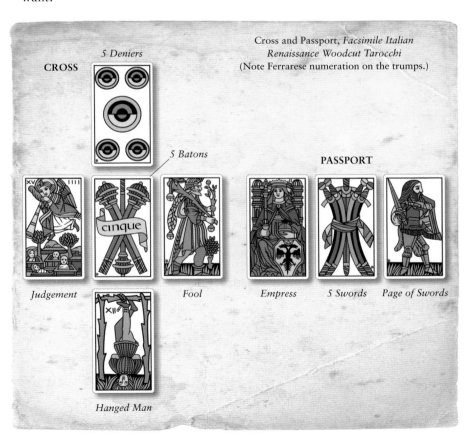

CROSS

5 Deniers

Cross and Passport, *Facsimile Italian Renaissance Woodcut Tarocchi* (Note Ferrarese numeration on the trumps.)

5 Batons

PASSPORT

Judgement

Fool

Empress

5 Swords

Page of Swords

Hanged Man

The Passport
Reading the three cards as the way forward.

Empress, 5 Swords, Page of Swords = it is a woman's feminine wisdom to change this aggressive risk of this boyfriend. If this isn't clear enough, we can also mirror the Passport cards with the corresponding Three in the Cross to confirm a reading: here, I've chosen to read the mirroring as 1 + 6, 2 + 7, 3 + 9.

Judgement + Empress = a woman who gets the return of a boyfriend for whom she longs.

5 Batons + 5 Swords = struggle and rivalry are involved in her getting her heart's wish.

Fool + Page of Swords = the boyfriend is still going to be both vacillating and aggressive.

To compound this reading, there are also three Fives present, showing that she will be struggling with challenges as a result of getting her boyfriend back. The missing Five here is 5 Cups: love is significantly absent. This is a case of "be careful what you wish for" – these cards spoke so clearly that the querent was seriously challenged in her desire to have her boyfriend back. I gave her the number of a woman's hostel should things get tough, but in the end it was her decision.

The Pyramid Spread

```
              ┌─────┐
              │     │
              │  1  │
              │     │
              └─────┘

    ┌─────┐          ┌─────┐
    │     │          │     │
    │  2  │          │  3  │
    │     │          │     │
    └─────┘          └─────┘

┌─────┐      ┌─────┐      ┌─────┐
│     │      │     │      │     │
│  4  │      │  5  │      │  6  │
│     │      │     │      │     │
└─────┘      └─────┘      └─────┘
```

This Pyramid shows the following:

Card 1 The issue.
Cards 2 and 3 The factors or dynamics playing out in it.
Cards 4–6 How the issue is dealt with.
You can also read 1 + 5 to discover something that is unknown or hidden.

In this example, taken from my tarot notebook, I was asking what I needed to be aware of before I set out to officiate at a wedding, at a venue unknown to me.

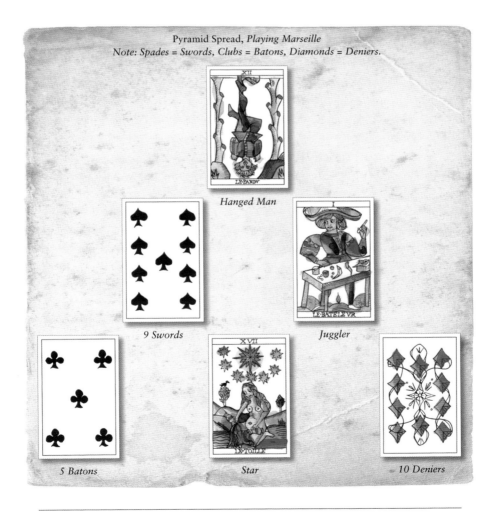

Pyramid Spread, *Playing Marseille*
Note: *Spades = Swords, Clubs = Batons, Diamonds = Deniers.*

Hanged Man

9 Swords   Juggler

5 Batons   Star   10 Deniers

Hanged Man It looks as if I will be hanging around a good deal.
9 Swords + Juggler This combination speaks to me about "dangerous staging."
5 Batons + Star + 10 Deniers Quite a bit of physical preparation will be needed so that the dream wedding will be satisfactory for the family.
Hanged Man + Star This feels like a delayed blessing, which makes me anxious. I will set out early, just in case.

And here is what I found, as recorded afterwards in my notebook:

"Later: After arriving at the outdoor venue very early – and it was as well I had done so – I found that the seating area was sited on very soft ground with a thin groundsheet covering hundreds of mole-holes. With the ushers, I was able to warn guests in high heels to remove their shoes while walking on this area, and for myself I reverted to sandals rather than the heeled shoes I'd been intending to wear. Due to rain the night before, I also had to move quite a few chairs by myself. The Hanged Man and Star combination proved to have been saying 'long drawn-out blessing,' as the couple wanted to add a last-minute blessing ritual to what was already a very full ceremony."

Always follow up your reading with a report as to what befell. This way, you can check the accuracy of your own reading.

The Fountain Spread

This method is a good way of strengthening your reading of simple card combinations without using any predetermined positions. The Fountain Spread uses the interconnecting triads as the means of reading the cards. In each case, the underlying cards of each triad's base speak about, describe or amplify the card that makes the apex of the triangle. Try it for yourself.

Card 1 The issue under question.
Cards 2 and 3 Speak about card 1.
Cards 4 and 5 Speak about card 2.
Cards 5 and 6 Amplify card 3.
Cards 7 and 8 Amplify card 4.
Cards 8 and 9 Amplify card 5.
Cards 9 and 10 Amplify card 6.

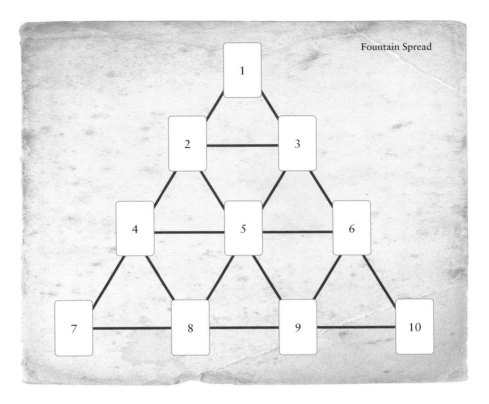

Fountain Spread

If the story is still running, your fountain can spill further on; if it stops earlier, then stop when you have the picture. For a final word, in the event of anything that is unclear, or when you need to confirm the message, you can read cards 7 and 10 as amplifying card 1. Additionally, if you need to understand the dynamic at work in these cards, you can read the three internal reversed triads of 2, 3 and 5; 4, 5 and 8; and 5, 6 and 9, although this is rarely necessary.

CHAPTER 6

THE ART OF DIRECTIONAL READING

Only mix, and do not tire,
Turn and shuffle yet again,
Move it, reverse it,
And then turn once more.
If to the right,
It is not right for you.
With the left,
In the kitchen, as you will,
For left-handed is to be praised,
Just as in Tarocchino,
For the ladies, it's a new fashion.

GIROLAMO BARUFFALDI (1675–1755), *The Sauces*, Bacchanal V, translated by Caitlín Matthews

SIGNIFICATORS

The saucy verse above comments on the way fashionable ladies laid out their tarot cards, but it can also refer to how the figures on your cards face to one side or the other. Directional reading, or the skill of reading from the way in which cards are facing towards or away from each other, is a major tool in making sense of the untold story. One of the first things that we need to explore before going on to look at it more closely is the significator, which will help us to learn more about directionality.

A significator is a card chosen to represent the querent; in modern readings, this card is usually chosen from the courts, and is removed from the pack and set aside, but leaving it sitting on the table without moving is like driving in neutral gear, so we are going to use ours in a more powerful way by leaving it in the pack. Significators were present in playing card divination from at least the early 17th century onwards, with many references to the court cards being so used. In the 1770s, Etteilla designated the first specific significator card in his *Petit Etteilla*, where a blank card or carte blanche, modestly called "Etteilla," after himself, serves this function.[64] When he created his *Book of Thoth* tarot, he assigned card number 1 to be the male significator or male questioner and card 8 to be the female questioner. These appear to take the places of the Popess and Pope cards of the *Tarot de Marseille*, which Etteilla chose to rework and renumber. A significator enables us to see what the querent is facing or ignoring, but how do we chose one?

In Chapter 3, we read how Paulmy d'Argenson assigned the playing card ranks and suits to people: the King represented an adult man, the Queen a woman, while the Valet/Page was a young person.[65] In times past, it was customary to see each of the courts as male or female, and to determine which would be a good significator by assigning hair color to each of the courts:

COURT	SWORDS	BATONS	CUPS	DENIERS
Page Child/youth with	Brown hair	Blond/red hair	Light brown hair	Dark hair
Knight Young man with	Brown hair	Blond/red hair	Light brown hair	Dark hair
Queen Woman with	Brown hair	Blond/red hair	Light brown hair	Dark/grey hair
King Older man with	Brown hair	Blond/red hair	Light brown hair	Dark/grey hair

The Hermetic Order of the Golden Dawn further associated the pips and courts with the decans or divisions of the zodiac, as well as assigning kabbalistic and astrological associations to the trumps. This has led many modern readers to choose significators according to the querent's astrological sign or other factors. The more recent trend is to create less stereotypical distinctions; many modern tarots now have asexual, inclusive, interracial or more integrated court cards. Yet, in the *Cary-Yale Visconti Sforza* tarot there are two Pages and two Knights, one of each sex, in each suit; in the *Minchiate* tarots, the *Fante* or Pages of Cups and Deniers are usually female, while the *Fanti* or Pages of Swords and Batons are male.[66] Taromancers who base their interpretation on psychology also now work with the Myers-Briggs personality types, based upon Jungian designations.[67]

Each of the historic tarot court cards faces to one side or the other, and thus they are most suitable as a pool of possible significators. When you have learned the sixteen courts, you can, of course, apply their characteristics to anyone of either sex. Your boss may be a woman but if she is clearly a King of Deniers, then cast her so! He may be a mummy's boy but casting him as

Queen of Cups is really fine. Return to Chapter 4 and decide which court card suits you best as a significator.

Mirror Pairs

In this simple cut, you can immediately check what a querent is bringing you to read about, and you can also practice your sense of direction.

1 Decide which court is the querent's significator.
2 Shuffle and cut your tarot into two. Examine both piles to see where the significator has landed, but without taking it out of the pile. Note how many cards up or down it is in the sequence.
3 Now look through the other pile, counting the same number up or down, and remove that card: this is the mirror to your significator.
4 How do the two cards relate to each other? Do they face each other or back on to each other?
5 If one or both is facing outwards, add another card/s to see what they are looking at.

This example (below) was drawn for a woman who lives alone: she is represented by the Queen of Swords. I drew these cards the day before I read for her, to get the lie of the land. The mirror card is the Pope. She is cold-shouldering religious authority, or she is out of favor with it; perhaps it is mutual? To find out, since both are looking outwards in this pair, I add a card at each end.

Mirror Pairs, *Tarot de Marseille Pierre Madenié 1709*

10 Swords	World	Queen of Swords	Pope	Knight of Swords
4	3	1	2	5

Now, the Pope is blessing the Knight of Swords and the Queen of Swords is looking anxiously at the World. Because of a man whose actions have been motivated by his church, rather than his heart, the woman is estranged from both him and his church. She has sought out other means of belonging, but it worries her. Since the World is also facing left, I add another card, 10 Swords. The world has proved a dangerous place for her and she is overwhelmed with paranoia. This closes the line and we have a mini-story that gives me an impression of what we are dealing with. Notice that, although we started with two cards, we end up with a line of five cards, having compiled the story *in the order in which we uncovered the cards*. When I saw her the next day, this story was sadly confirmed. She had become estranged from a very exacting man and their shared spiritual beliefs a long while ago. She was now virtually agoraphobic and had become a hoarder for whom time had stopped, defensively fending off the world.

In any line, you can add an additional card to any card that faces out of the line at either end, as we shall see.

Reading in the Direction of the Significator

Historic decks have well-defined direction, with their figures looking to right or left. Following on from how we identify and use the significator, we turn to a skill that comes from the *Tarocchino Bolognese* method of reading. As we have seen, the main stars of significator reading are the sixteen courts. The direction in which the subjects on the cards look affects how we read. This line-of-sight method, whereby the gaze of the card looks towards the left or right, can highlight things that the client hasn't seen.

In the picture overleaf, the chosen significator is the Page of Batons who looks to the reader's left: the cards are read in a line. In this traditional method, the normal left–right direction of reading is reversed, so that the cards are laid right to left, following where the Page of Batons is looking. Here you combine the traditional skill of line-reading with the method of reading directionally, according to the significator's point of view, which gives you an authentic untold story. In this instance, the client is a thirty-year-old man who has just had some alarming news and wants to know how it will play out. As the Page of Batons, he is looking at 10 Cups to his left, followed by the Moon, the King of Cups, 10 Deniers, Pope (in this tarot he is Capitano Eracasse), Tower, Popess (in this tarot, Bacchus) and Knight of Swords.

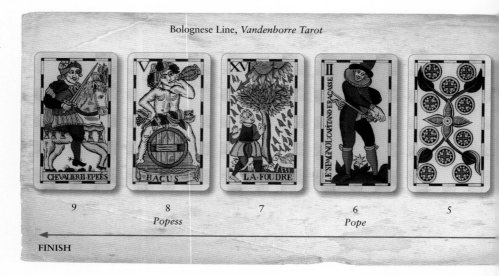

Bolognese Line, *Vandenborre Tarot*

9   8   7   6   5

Popess   *Pope*

FINISH

What does the Page of Batons see? Blending 10 Cups with the Moon suggests an accident, with much loss of blood. The King of Cups is next to this accident: it is an older man who has suffered this and I guess it is the client's father, which he confirms. The King of Cups looks towards 10 Deniers, which is combined with the Pope and the Tower, which can also signify a building. There is family sorrow here, as the father has to go into hospital. The Popess and Knight of Swords together show us that the father will need an operation.

Here, I have drawn upon modern *Tarocchino Bolognese* meanings, which have evolved from the Pratesi list on page 31. This tradition strongly blends cards to provide other meanings, as you learned in Chapter 5. Note that we have two Ten cards, showing us that we are looking at a crisis. The Tower, shown as a lightning-struck person, between the two papal cards which here in the *Vandenborre Tarot* are characteristically demoted, respectively, to the roistering Captain and Bacchus, reveal a life-or-death situation.

Messengers of News

In order to learn this skill of reading in the direction that the significator is looking, try this simple method of discovering the upcoming news as a forecast. Traditionally, the four Pages represent messengers, so here you will use them to discover the course of your life in the next week or month. They each face one direction or another and will seek out that news for you. Here are the types of news they speak about:

The arrow shows the reading direction from the Page of Batons to the Knight of Swords.

START READING HERE

Page of Swords Work, business, ambitions, plans
Page of Batons Social events, projects, enthusiasms, interests
Page of Cups Domestic issues, family or romantic events
Page of Deniers Finance, responsibilities, embodying plans

1 Shuffle your pack thoroughly while considering your question: "What news is there of my next week/month?"

2 Turn the pack upright and look through it to find where the four Pages are located, without pulling them out. Simply lift the cards proud of the main pack, like bookmarks, until all have been found.

3 Lay the pack on a flat surface, spreading it out carefully, and check which cards the Pages are facing. Using their individual lines of sight, select the sequence of cards that they are looking at to read the news for yourself: 2–5 cards will suffice. (The example overleaf only has three cards for each Page.)

4 Lay out each sequence and read the cards. The cards that each Page regards will speak about the nature of the news. Trumps may speak about momentous events, while courts will show who you will be meeting, and pip cards will reveal the details.

5 Occasionally, of course, the Pages speak about each other and you will sometimes find that one Page is facing another Page, suggesting that the news they each bring will be about each other's business: a combination of responsibility and pleasure.

Here, a woman is looking ahead to the next few weeks, asking to see what she will be dealing with. In this example, each Page is accompanied by the three cards that it looks towards – you could choose up to five cards if you feel that the sequence they are each looking at warrants it. Sometimes the statement that the cards make speaks succinctly and only two cards are required. As you will see, the Pages in this *Giacomo Zoni Tarot* all face left, except for the Page of Batons who looks right. Although reading from right to left may be unfamiliar, try it and see for yourself. Blend the cards as you go.

All cards are listed below in the positions in which they appear in the layout. Remember that we begin with the Page in each line and read the cards in the direction the Page is facing; the arrow denotes the directional order of reading. I have also broken down each card and shown how the blending works.

Line 1: World • Justice • 7 Swords ⟵ *Page of Swords*
The Page of Swords speaks about work, business, ambitions and plans. The 7 Swords is in a state of negotiation with Justice, who governs the truth and integrity of things, while the World is about attainment. Together, they blend to say, "Deeply analyzing the plan, so that it can be achieved and brought into public consciousness." The woman will be working on assembling her plans into an ordered blueprint, so that she can share her ambitious plans with others.

Line 2: Ace of Deniers • 5 Cups • Knight of Deniers ⟵ *Page of Cups*
The Page of Cups is concerned with domestic issues, family or romantic events. He immediately faces the Knight of Deniers riding towards him, who represents a shrewd, experienced older man. Behind the Knight is 5 Cups, which combines struggle with love, while the Ace of Deniers is about primal resources. Together, they blend to say, "The woman will meet up with her older lover and they have a lovers' argument about the use of resources." This disagreement could equally be about shared use of money or space.

Line 3: *Page of Batons* ⟶ 9 Cups • Devil • 4 Deniers
The Page of Batons brings news of social events, projects, enthusiasms or interests. He is looking at 9 Cups, traditionally "the wish card." However, it is followed by the Devil, who challenges or stagnates things, giving those wishes a different cast. The 4 Deniers, which might be welcome as an orderly card of physical circumstances, doesn't serve the client so well when blended with the foregoing cards. They say, "The project you most want to come to fruition presents itself in a way that circumscribes enjoyment of it." It rather looks as if

Messengers of News, *Giacomo Zoni Tarot*

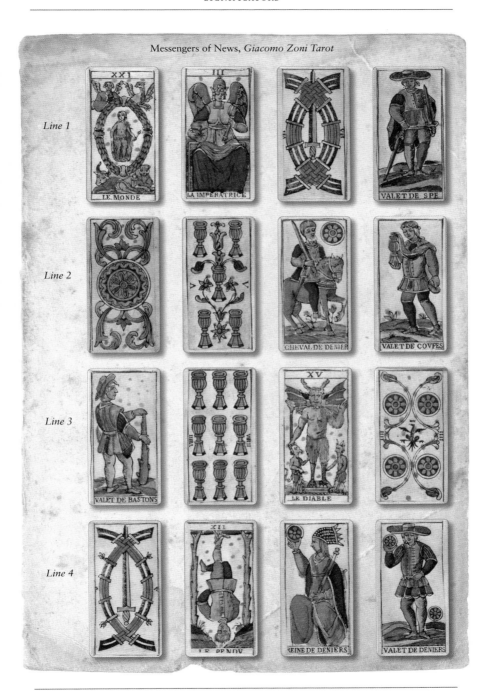

Line 1

Line 2

Line 3

Line 4

Devil and 4 Deniers create a stagnating box for this project: there either won't be enough money for it, or the conditions attached to its enjoyment are limited.

LINE 4: 5 Swords • Hanged Man • Queen Deniers ⟵ *Page of Deniers*
The Page of Deniers brings news of finance, responsibilities and how things are manifested or embodied. He looks at the Queen of Deniers, who has her back turned to him: she enables things to be done well, and could be a colleague or friend of the client, even her mother – a can-do woman. She looks towards Hanged Man, who can signify betrayal or punitive action, and 5 Swords, which includes divisive thoughts or anxieties. They combine to say, "The older woman has to deal with betrayal and worry," which the client will have to help shoulder.

Assemble your own Pages to bring you the news. Look back at your findings at the end of the chosen period you were reading about and check to see how the news played out. For example, in the reading above, the woman did work hard on her work plans but, as the Page of Batons said, the frame into which all her hopes fell wasn't as ample as she would have wished. The lovers' argument was about how she and her boyfriend might share a home together, but it worked out amicably, while the Page of Deniers was talking about the client's unstable brother who had stolen from their mother, causing her no end of anxiety.

Which Way do the Card Subjects Face?

If you lay out the trumps of a historic tarot and those of the *Rider Waite-Smith* deck beside each other, you will notice a curious thing. The figures on the cards of a historic tarot like the *Tarot de Marseille* not only face in different directions but they are also figures that you would never see in daily life because they depict archetypal beings. However, the *Rider Waite-Smith* trumps, although they illustrate similar archetypes, largely look forwards and, with the exception of Death, are all looking like people you might meet in the street. The difference between the older and later decks is largely one of consciousness: we no longer respect the archetypes in the trumps as once we did from a civil, political or religious perspective. We have developed in consciousness until we can look upon Justice, the Tower or the Popess without demur or a shudder. The archetypes in modern tarots now look like ordinary people.

In most modern tarots, cards have a tendency to look straight at you, behaving like mirrors of the viewer's personality or reflecting some part of their soul. Such directness and intimacy is perhaps somewhat overwhelming when you are divining. The older tarots retain a courtesy and interrelation with each other, within which we can all be included.

Historic tarots are not psychological but archetypal in the Platonic sense: essences of principles. Each trump comes with its symbols that proclaim this: the keys of the Popess and the Pope that open the gates of heaven; the sword and balances of Justice that wield punishment or protection to the weak, or which weigh guilt and innocence. But each of the trumps and courts also has a stance or gesture which gives agency and movement to the figure. By noticing what the figures in the cards are looking at, we can learn further things.

In *Tarot de Marseille,* the only front-facing figures are Hanged Man, Justice, Devil, Sun and Judgement: respectively, we could say, with scripture, that none are exempt from punishment; justice is for all; the Devil prowls to see whom he can devour; the sun shines on the just and unjust; and all receive judgement. These five cards seem related to the doctrine of the *Four Last Things* from Catholic eschatology – the four final experiences that everyone must face: Death, Judgement, Heaven or Hell. Death is not in this line-up of cards because it faces to the right, but Justice and Judgement together represent the Last Judgement, which ascertains one's soul's destination; the Devil represents Hell, the Sun represents Heaven (Christ is called the Son cf. St John 8:12, "I am the Light of the World" and Psalms 84:11 "The Lord God is a Sun"); while the Hanged Man represents Purgatory, the place of purification.

When you see any of these front-facing cards in a line reading, I suggest that you draw two cards and place one above and one below it, to get a sense of what they are showing you, as here, in this line of five, where a man asks what will be the outcome of a proposed publishing decision which is going to radically change the nature of his book. He draws two of the face-forward cards, so I add a pair of two cards, one above and below both Justice and Hanged Man (see page 180).

As we can see, the line has a rather uncompromising feel, beginning and ending in two of the face-forward cards. A judgement is being made about a primary outlay of money on this book: a design decision to beautify or enhance the book seriously compromises what the author wants, so that he feels literally strung up. We look at what the additional cards have to add: in the publisher's mind, the author is creating a silly fuss. The King of Batons under Justice is likely to represent the author, and shows that the decision will not be to his advantage. Over Hanged Man we have 5 Cups – a discordant relationship – while under it is the Lovers – the card of choice and relationship. The author is unlikely to call the shots in this annoying change.

(*Continues on page 182.*)

Building the Story from the Gaze (i), *CBD Tarot de Marseille*

A line of five with two front-facing cards, with
their two additional cards (marked here in italic).
The numbers under each card show the order
in which cards were laid, while the arrows
indicate the figure's gaze.

Fool
6 →

5 Cups
8

Justice
1

Ace of Deniers
2

Empress
3 →

2 Swords
4

Hanged Man
5

King of Batons
7 →

Lovers
← 9

Building the Story from the Gaze (ii), *CBD Tarot de Marseille*

Additional cards in the direction of the gaze (again, marked here in italic).

Fool
6 →

5 Deniers
10

5 Cups
8

Justice
1

Ace of Deniers
2

Empress
3 →

2 Swords
4

Hanged Man
5

King of Batons
7 →

10 Cups
11

8 Cups
12

Lovers
← 9

An additional method is to see where the figure cards are looking and to add a card in the direction of their gaze, if there is a space to do so. We don't do this with Empress, as she is already looking at 2 Swords. Three more cards help us to follow the gaze of the figure cards now (see page 181).

The Fool looks towards 5 Deniers: yet another Five shows us that there are arguments over money. The King of Batons looks at 10 Cups: his cherished fulfillment. We could also read each of the first, second and third columns as a statement:

Fool, Justice, King of Batons "Wayward" is how the author is judged.
5 Deniers, Ace of Deniers, 10 Cups Arguments about the money offset his fulfillment.
5 Cups, Hanged Man, Lovers Bad feeling restricts the author because of this choice.

Following the gaze of the man in the Lovers card, we place 8 Cups: the decision breaks the author's trust in his publisher.

This reading has no good news for the author and it looks as if the publisher will plough on regardless, however we read it, but I hope you can see from this placement and reading of directional cards how you can prise open and reveal dynamics you had not seen, and skillfully unfold the story.

Tableau Reading

We have seen how significators can act when they fall in lines, but they come into their own when we look at tableau reading. A tableau is "a picture"; it is still one of the more powerful methods of divining because, having laid out a square or rectangle of cards, we can pinpoint precisely where the querent is in the issue. Tableaux, although they are the most traditional ways of laying cards, look troubling to the modern taromancer's eye as they contain so many cards but, be assured, we read them selectively here. Where the significator shows up in the tableau tells us a lot: the position they land on, the cards that surround them, the direction that they're facing, the card they've turned their back on, the whole hidden agenda.

Tableau reading is what is most often depicted in paintings of cartomancy, like this image of playing cards laid in tableau in Alfred Russo's *The Card Reader c.*1913–19 (see opposite). The cards are laid in ranks and become a map which the taromancer can read.

Tableau reading from Alfred Russo's *The Card Reader*

Tableau of Twenty-five

In his *Memoires*, the libertine Casanova tells us that his young mistress, Zaïre, jealously accused him of his debaucheries by laying "a square of twenty-five cards wherein she makes me read all the debaucheries that had kept me out all night long."[68] After her detailed reading, which is unfortunately not given, Casanova heaved her pack of cards into the fire in disgust. Here is a tableau of twenty-five and how to read one, enabling you to discover the precise nature of an issue by giving you the surrounding landscape of the story, allowing you to glimpse where the querent is within their story.

1 Shuffle in your pre-selected significator and divide the pack into three piles of twenty-six cards each. Look through each pile to find which one the significator is in, without changing the order of the cards.

2 Discarding the other two piles, lay out only the significator pile of twenty-six cards into five rows of five cards each, placing the twenty-sixth card either in the row nearest to the significator or at the edge if it has fallen there, as in the example overleaf. (If the significator falls as the twenty-sixth card, start again from process 1 above.) This card shows how the querent is facing the question or it acts as an ally or the querent's conscience.

3 Note where the significator falls in the ranks. Each horizontal row gives us a clue as to the querent's condition. In the top row, the querent is at the top of his game; in the second row, he's still pretty good; in row three,

things are middling; in row four, it's beginning to be poor; in row five, things are not good.

4 The columns reveal where the querent is in her story: in column one, she is just starting out, while in column five, her story is coming to an end. The columns can also be related to time, with the column in which the significator has fallen being "now," the ones to its left the nearer or further past, and the ones to the right the nearer or further future.

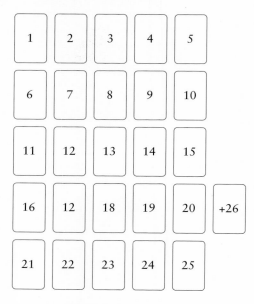

5 Look over the whole tableau and note any clumps of cards that sing out immediately, then turn to the breakdown. There are many ways of reading what is there, including:

- ⊙ Read the diagonal corners as a statement: 1 + 25 and 5 + 21.
  This gives the outline of the story.
- ⊙ Read the cross of cards above, below and either side of the significator.
  If it is at an edge, use the extra card to complete the cross.
  What's above, below, to the left and right of the significator?
- ⊙ Check the pivot card in the central, thirteenth position. This shows the issue's origin or fixation.
- ⊙ Check the diagonals leading to and from the significator.
- ⊙ Read the inner cross – 8, 12, 14, 18 – and the outer cross – 3, 11, 15, 23.
- ⊙ Check the knighting (see page 188).

Overleaf is a tableau I did for a woman in Europe whose husband had disappeared from home and failed to appear at work. It was read in the period before the police would agree to institute a search so, although I would not normally accept a third-party reading, this was clearly an emergency. This family had immense problems, while the man himself had addictive patterns and many challenges. A few days later his body was found by the police in his car where he'd committed suicide.

I invite you to study this tableau with respect and compassion, and without judgement. Please also note that the Death card did not appear in the tableau, although death resulted, as we can infer from the subject's position.

The illustration on page 186 shows the man's pre-selected significator, marked in green: King of Swords. It's located at the very bottom of the tableau, and his card is looking at Judgement. We also note that the extra card is 2 Batons: this is a man who is facing up to work challenges and looking into eternity. These are the cards that were drawn:

Ace of Swords	Popess	6 Batons	10 Swords	6 Swords
Chariot	Pope	2 Swords	Page of Deniers	3 Cups
Ace of Batons	10 Deniers	Queen of Cups	Justice	Queen of Batons
Temperance	Sun	8 Cups	8 Batons	9 Cups
Moon	7 Swords	Knight of Deniers	King of Swords	Judgement
			2 Batons	

The corners frame the story: Ace of Swords, Judgement, 6 Swords, Moon. His mental health is under sentence, as plans fail to work out amid confusion and anxiety. Significantly, we cannot read the entire square of the missing man because it is in the corner, at the edge: the story literally runs out. All we can see is that he has 8 Batons over his head, making him feel trapped by his job; the Knight of Deniers to his left tells us that he is impelled by forceful action; Judgement is to his right, which he also faces squarely as if determined to give things another go. The extra card beneath him, 2 Batons, is the traditional card for "a short space of time," and this worried me because, when associated with these others, it felt as if precipitate action was happening, even as I read.

The center card as pivot in the middle, the Queen of Cups, is very much connected with the two other female figures of Justice and the Queen of Batons, who I judged was the subject's wife, as we'll see shortly in the knighting on page 188. Knighting is a way of associating one card with another through the knight's move in chess: two cards away horizontally and one card

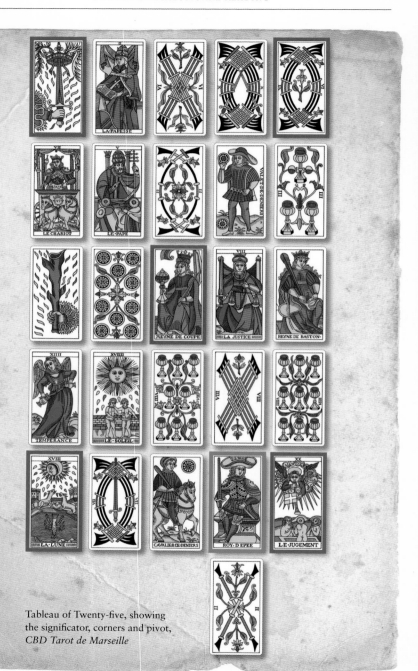

Tableau of Twenty-five, showing
the significator, corners and pivot,
CBD Tarot de Marseille

vertically, or two cards vertically and one card horizontally. His significator associates with the stability and kindness that his wife gave to him, and which largely kept him going. But these three female figures seem to sit glued together like the Fates.

The significator also knights the Sun, his search for happiness. Significantly, it is next to Temperance – the challenge of addiction he struggled with for most of his life: his sense of failure in this and other regards was clearly a factor. Temperance itself knights the Knight of Deniers and the Queen of Cups: the Knight of Deniers seems to represent his disturbed son, who has similar problems to his father, while the Queen of Cups feels like an ungiving woman who has not provided the nurturing for this family, and who perhaps set up this addictive pattern: not the subject's wife, but his mother.

The first card in the tableau, the Ace of Swords, in the left corner knights 2 Swords: this is a classic combination about mental health or being in two minds, which can indicate a bipolar condition, although his wife said he had no such diagnosis. The man's dilemma had clearly been going on for some time, and his mind hung in the balance.

On page 189, we see the mirroring. This is a way of seeing which cards are associated together by seeing which ones occupy similar positions on the opposite sides of the tableau. We can do this with any card in this tableau except the pivot. It is as if we folded the tableau in half lengthways or widthways. The significator mirrors 10 Swords, 7 Swords and Popess: the man's worst fears play out, crushing his self-belief; it felt to me that he had withdrawn himself. His wife, the Queen of Batons, mirrors the Ace of Batons and 6 Batons, suggesting that she is involved with an educational building (she is a teacher); she also mirrors the Knight of Deniers, who is her very disturbed son. We note, too, that the significator turns his back to his son, who has proved too troublesome.

The diagonal line leading to the man – Chariot, 10 Deniers and 8 Cups – says "driven to embezzle the trust." This line suggested why he might have taken himself off, as he was fearful of what would be revealed, since he worked in finance. We did not know he was dead when I read, though I feared he might have done something precipitate. Afterwards, the man's widow had little idea of what had caused his suicide, since he had kept his worries secret, but she knew he had been troubled.

The location where the man was sadly found a few days later was a disused railway crossing, in his car. When I returned to look at the tableau, I noticed that it had actually told us the correct location: it can be clearly seen from the

(Continues on page 190.)

The Knighting,
CBD Tarot de Marseille

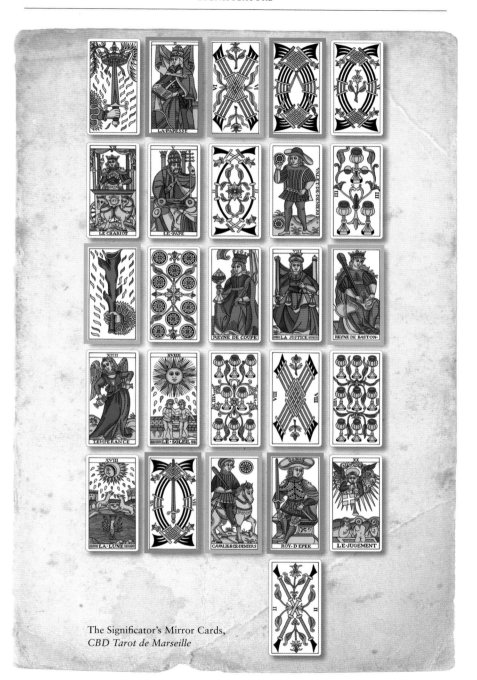

The Significator's Mirror Cards,
CBD Tarot de Marseille

knighting of Chariot with 6 Batons: car/vehicle and crossroads. We note that Chariot has the Ace of Swords above and the Ace of Batons below: a destructive and decisive action taken in a vehicle.

Here, I have not read all the cards: it isn't necessary, but you may find other things if you examine the tableau, especially the central nine cards surrounding the Queen of Cups. His wife later told me that her husband believed firmly in reincarnation; she took comfort that his gazing at Judgement here showed his faith that things would work out better another time.

Card-sifting

We have seen in the Tableau of Twenty-five on the previous pages that initial card-sifting to find where the significator has fallen can result in a tight, eloquent reading. You can start with fewer cards, of course. By putting the significator into the pack, and enabling it to come back into the reading, you are able to make it work harder. If you do not wish to lose any card's value from your tarot, you can make your own carte blanche as a universal significator by cutting out a piece of card the same size as your tarot, just as Etteilla did.

Significators can be shuffled into the pack and then all the cards are dealt out into piles, creating the basis for many different kinds of reading, as we saw above. By reading *only* the pile in which the significator has fallen, you limit the number of cards read. Some siftings reduce the tarot to a round number, but others result in one or more cards being left out of the deal: these can be set aside, becoming a group of advisers who can be called upon to amplify the reading, if necessary. If you wish to create a spread that enables this kind of reading, here is how seventy-eight cards break down into piles:

- 3 piles x 26 cards each = 78
- 4 piles x 19 cards each = 76 + 2 extra
- 6 piles x 13 cards each = 78
- 7 piles x 11 cards each = 77 + 1 extra
- 8 piles x 9 cards each = 72 + 6 extra
- 10 piles x 7 cards each = 70 + 8 extra
- 13 piles x 6 cards each = 78

The significator pile can be laid in lines, if it contains between six and eleven cards, as shown opposite.

Creating Significator Readings
for 6–11 cards

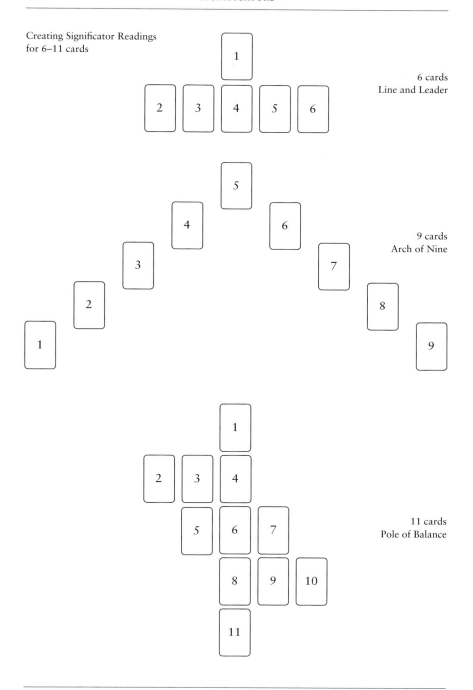

6 cards
Line and Leader

9 cards
Arch of Nine

11 cards
Pole of Balance

Between thirteen and twenty-six cards can be laid out in different ways: the arch also enables you to mirror cards with each other, with the center card as a hinge, as on page 189.

Tableau Shapes for 13–26 cards

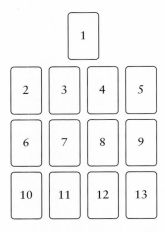

13 Card Tableau

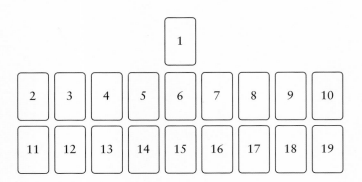

19 Card Tableau

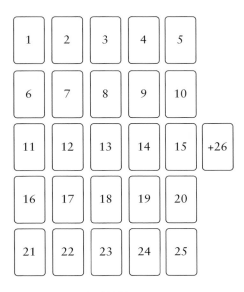

26 Card Tableau

Where the significator falls in any spread or tableau can help you read the untold story: What are they looking at or avoiding? What precedes or follows them? What are they mirroring or knighting? What is over their heads, beneath their feet and to either side? Lay your cards and find out.

CHAPTER 7

Telling the Untold Story

✦

I always play taroccho and tarocchi.
To me it is ever wondrous, ever new,
And I get angry when someone says:
"You never notice the passing of the day and hour."

GIOVAN BATTISTA FAGIUOLI (1660–1742), *Verses*, translated by Caitlín Matthews

THE OLDEST SPREADS

The addictive power of tarot is well known among taromancers: hours can go by, indeed, as we follow where the story leads us. The world has now been playing tarot in one form or another for many hundreds of years, and here I share two of the oldest spreads in existence, both from the mid 18th century, for you to try for yourself. With these and the spreads that follow, you can bring together the skills you have learned here.

The Pratesi Sheet Spread

The list of tarocchino meanings from 1750 (see page 31) also gives a method of laying just the cards in the list: "If cards are laid in five piles, it will ensure there will be seven cards in each pile." [69] Using only the cards in the Pratesi list – fifteen trumps (without the Wheel, Justice, the two papal or imperial figures and Tower), the courts (leaving out the Queen, Knight and Page of Swords), and just four Aces and three Tens (leaving out 10 Batons) – you have your pack ready to go.

We have no instructions as to what the five piles signified, so you can create your own criteria for this: each can represent aspects of the querent's issue, or they can represent health, wealth, luck, work/prospects and family. A spread of thirty-five cards seems a lot to a modern reader, but you can read these speedily using brief cartomantic meanings or keywords. Try it first with just the meanings on page 31 and see how it plays out, as this is a rare opportunity to use a historic spread together with its original meanings. Afterwards, try this method using thirty-five cards dealt from the full pack and one of your favored reading methods.

Five Bolognese Piles / Seven-card Pile, *Tarocchi Fine Dalla Torre in Bologna*

Ace of Batons	Hanged Man	Queen of Deniers	King of Batons	10 Cups	World	King of Cups
The house	Betrayal	Truth	Single man	Roof tiles	Long journey	Old man

If you have but a short time, then choose which of the seven-card piles will speak most eloquently to you: under the seven-card example shown above, I have placed the corresponding Pratesi keywords.

The middle card in the line is the King of Batons, a single man, so let us read it as his story: "The household is in uproar when a betrayal by an unmarried man comes to light. No longer welcome under that roof, he departs for a long journey, only returning when he is old."

If we mirror the cards as the King of Batons' story, we get:

Ace of Batons + King of Cups = the house belongs to an older man.
Hanged Man + World = betrayal is what sets the young man on his journey.
Queen of Deniers + 10 Cups = truth expels him from the shelter of the household.

Here, the mirroring cards confirm what we first found, but we see a possible sharpening of the original assessment of him coming home only when he is old: perhaps he only returns home when the householder himself dies.

Grimpetto's Spread

This spread dates from about 1730 and was originally used with the *Tarocchino Bolognese* cards, but you can use your own tarot. Immediately, we are struck by what an inquisitive and unethical spread it is: today, most taromancers are reluctant to do what are referred to as "third-party" readings – those which enquire about, or on behalf of, others. Nevertheless, despite all its problematic surveillance issues, here it is. I suggest that you use a fictional character to understand how it works.

Grimpetto's Spread showing the order of card layout 1–15

B *What is in their head*

C *What is in their heart*　　　　　　　　　　　**D** *What is disagreeable to them*

A *What is in their breast*

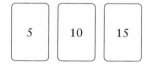

E *What is trampled upon*

The positions signify:

A The subject's emotions.
B The subject's thoughts.
C What opens the subject's heart in an expansive way.
D What closes the subject's heart in a disagreeable way.
E The things that they do not want to confront or cannot see.

1 Decide on a (fictional) character you want to learn more about. Choose a male or female significator card and lay it centrally. It is traditional to "baptize" or name the card, which is called "The Witness," as the character it represents.

2 Place one card over it at the position of *Breast*, one above for *Head*, one to the left for *Heart*, one to the right for the *Flank*, one below for what is *Underfoot*. As you deal out one card at a time into positions A–E, it is traditional to say, in turn, "In the breast, in the head, in the heart, on the flank, underfoot." The three middle cards slightly cover The Witness.

3 Keep laying one card per position, in this order, on the five piles, until there are three cards on each pile.

4 Read each triplet in its position.

Finding the Way Spread

This spread is helpful for a client who needs to make a decision but is unable to see the underlying issue or personal imperative. I devised it to bring together the skills you have learned in earlier chapters. We read the cards in a line, like a modern cinematic storyboard. Finally, the top and bottom vertical pairs are read together. As with many older spreads it requires numerous processes, so follow the unfolding sequence slowly until you have the full story.

The spread draws upon skills from the *Tarocchino Bolognese* method of reading where significators are always pre-set. So *any* female client is represented by the Queen of Batons and her thoughts by the Page of Batons, while *any* male client is represented by the King of Batons and his thoughts by the Knight of Batons. If you are used to using different significators for yourself and others, then simply set those aside and try this way for a change.

The cards follow the gaze of the querent's significator, while their thoughts are read in the direction in which they face. If, in your pack, the significator or thoughts cards look ahead rather than to the right or left, then read in whichever is your customary direction! Finally, each card in the top line is read as a pair with the card that mirrors it in the bottom line.

1 Shuffle your question into the deck and deal out all seventy-eight cards into eleven piles of seven cards each, with one card left over. The leftover card becomes *the theme of the reading*. Place this at the head of the spread, as the theme of the reading, at 0.

2 Check in which of the eleven piles is the significator: the Queen of Batons for a woman or the King of Batons for a man. Set this pile aside.

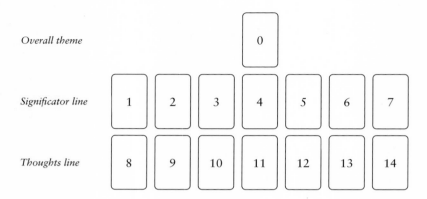

Overall theme 0

Significator line 1 2 3 4 5 6 7

Thoughts line 8 9 10 11 12 13 14

3 Check in which pile is the person's thoughts card: the Page of Batons for a woman or the Knight of Batons for a man. Set this pile aside also.

4 Now discard the unused piles. (Note: if your thoughts and significator cards *arrive in same pile together,* select a random pile, swop the thoughts card with any card from it, and then use this pile as the thoughts pile.)

5 Lay the significator pile in a line from cards 1 to 7.

6 Lay the thoughts pile in a line from 8 to 14.

7 Read the overall theme card at position 0 in the plan above.

8 Read the top line, *starting with the significator* and reading in the direction in which it gazes, treating the line as continuous. In the *Tarot de Marseille* the entire Batons suit looks left, but if you use a different tarot and your significator or thoughts card looks to the right, then that is how you will read the cards in that line.

9 Read the lower line from the querent's thoughts card, in the direction that it looks, continuing to the last card in the line.

10 Now read the vertical pairs, starting from the significator with the cards under it in order: 1 + 8, 2 + 9, and so on.

The cards shown opposite were drawn for a woman who heads up a family company: she is on the horns of a dilemma, having recently succeeded to the chair after her elder brother's sudden death. She did not expect to have to step up to public duty; her new position and her needs as a private person are clashing. How can she steer a way between them? The cards reveal the untold story.

Finding the Way, *Giacomo Zoni Tarot*

Pope

| 5 Cups | 4 Deniers | 8 Swords | Lovers | Queen of Batons | Page of Cups | 6 Swords |

| 3 Deniers | Page of Batons | Tower | King of Swords | Ace of Swords | 7 Batons | Judgement |

Theme card Pope. The theme is clearly set by this card: the Pope is the spiritual head, just as the client is supposed to be the inspirer and leader of the family firm. The expectations upon her are immense: she is on show to the whole world, having to set an example.

Line 1 is read from the significator, the Queen of Batons, who represents the client here. Even though it has fallen in position 5, we start from here. Since the Queen is facing right, we read from this card towards the end of the line and then go back to the beginning of the line, to position 1, to continue reading until we come to card 4. This line speaks about the client herself. In both lines in this spread, the story that the cards are telling sometimes runs from card to card; this is why contiguous statements sometimes come with dotted continuations below:

Card 5 Queen of Batons: The querent is looking at …

Card 6 Page of Cups, who faces her: there is a great willingness to be of service, but behind the Page's back is …

Card 7 6 Swords: … the integrity of her harmoniously ordered life which is clashing with …

Card 1 5 Cups: … the emotional struggle and disillusionment about her new post.

Card 2 4 Deniers: What everyone sees as a good stabilizing choice of a new executive who will lead the company to profit, in her eyes appears …

Card 3 8 Swords: … like a stressful restriction.

Card 4 Lovers: If she makes good choices, the querent can lead with a good sense of herself.

Line 2 is read from the card representing the client's thoughts, the Page of Batons, which has fallen in position 9. He is facing right, so we read to the end of the line at position 14 and return to the beginning of the line to read card 8. This line tells us about what the querent holds in her innermost thoughts, beliefs or assumptions about herself:

Card 9 Page of Batons: Her thoughts are fixated upon …

Card 10 Tower: the sudden devastation …

Card 11 King of Swords: … of her brother's passing. He was a very different person to her: expert and decisive. The weight of his loss together with …

Card 12 Ace of Swords: … the necessity to be the leader and instigator of the firm requires fresh resolve …

Card 13 7 Batons: … to explore the possibilities and pass beyond self-defensiveness.

Card 14 Judgement: By drawing the legacy of her brother and family, she can renew and refresh the company …

Card 8 3 Deniers: … by combining those family skills with her own creative ability, manifesting profit and grounding the work.

Reading the pairs This process of reading the cards of the top line with those of the bottom line enables the untold story to leap into focus. Start with the significator in the top row, reading it with the card beneath it. Look also at page 129 for pairing of suits.

Queen of Batons + Ace of Swords The issue preoccupying the client is like a sword of Damocles: it is ever-present and needs to be handled with great discernment. Batons with Swords requires her to have self-focus, suggesting that she is up for this challenge and that it is not beyond her.

Page of Cups + 7 Batons Her gentle style needs the energetic perseverance of 7 Batons to underscore it and give her some weight. Cups with Batons says she may find that she really enjoys this challenge.

6 Swords + Judgement In order to be a centralizing force in the firm, she has to draw upon ancestral values that have been long established. This will help to reboot her position in the firm, as well as to safeguard her own integrity.

5 Cups + 3 Deniers Her sense of disillusionment and emotional struggle can be tackled by investing herself in work: this will help her to feel less timid and unprepared.

4 Deniers + Page of Batons Stability will come when she engages her natural creativity. The pairing of Deniers with Batons also encourages her to discover how easy this is.

8 Swords + Tower She must remember that her struggle with this enforced change has come very suddenly and is accompanied by the devastating shock of her brother's death. She is deeply bereaved and will remain so for many months to come.

Lovers + King of Swords The choice before her is about negotiating the two halves of her work and personal life. She has the capacity to become more expert and established like her brother, but it will be with a more aesthetic touch than he could bring.

It is a steep learning curve for this woman, but she is more than able to face the challenge. Unsurprisingly, her sense of shock and bereavement are underscoring her new appointment. While the cards speak about her sudden immersion in the family firm and how she can work with it, they also reveal her innate sense of integrity and design, her love of beauty. In serving others, she doesn't have to forget to serve herself and her own needs.

The House of Triumphs Tableau

The House of Triumphs is a way of working with all twenty-two trumps in one tableau. We have already read a tableau without a predetermined set of positions, but here is one that modern readers can use with panache, in which each position is informed by the meaning of the trumps. The rooms in this house follow the sequence of the trumps as laid out in three lines, as shown here:

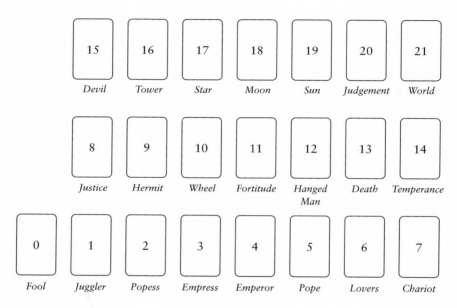

15	16	17	18	19	20	21
Devil	*Tower*	*Star*	*Moon*	*Sun*	*Judgement*	*World*

8	9	10	11	12	13	14
Justice	*Hermit*	*Wheel*	*Fortitude*	*Hanged Man*	*Death*	*Temperance*

0	1	2	3	4	5	6	7
Fool	*Juggler*	*Popess*	*Empress*	*Emperor*	*Pope*	*Lovers*	*Chariot*

Starting with the base line, we have trumps 1–7, with 8–14 in the middle line, and 15–21 at the top. Card 0, signifying the Fool's position, is the issue that is striving to enter the House of Triumphs. Each of these positions can be considered as rooms within the House, and each one takes the value of its card. So, if Justice lands on the room of the Moon at position 18, we can understand that the querent is having difficulty in discerning truth from illusion, or is striving to bring clarity to a confused or upsetting situation.

1 Separate the trumps from the rest of your pack and shuffle your question into them.
2 Lay out all twenty-two trumps randomly upon the rooms above, from position 0 to 21.

3 The card on position 0, at the threshold of the House, shows the main issue at work here.
4 Before checking which room each card has fallen into, examine any outstanding pairings, associations and combinations that speak out loudly. Sometimes parts of a line or a whole column will shriek their news at you.
5 While you can read all twenty-two cards, if you wish, the usual way of reading a tableau is to only scrutinize the significant cards for your issue.

In addition to reading specific issues and their relationship to the question, there are key positions where you can quickly see what is working out:

The card on position 0 shows the issue trying to gain entry into the House. Let's say we have the Chariot here, so the issue is about movement forward.

Check where the Fool has landed. This may reveal something that is unknown to the querent or show what the querent is currently tackling. If the Fool has landed on the Devil's room at position 15, the querent is in a state of self-sabotage or delusion.

The card in Room 11, at the center of the tableau, shows what is playing out here. It is the trigger or hidden motivation for the question.

The card in Room 20, the penultimate card, often shows the next step.

Note that cards that fall upon their own room, as in the sample reading overleaf, are confirmed in their effect. So, if Emperor lands in his own room, for example, his authority is strengthened or issues of authority are paramount.

Rooms in the House of the Triumphs

Using your own innate understanding of each trump, you can find auxiliary criteria that color the decor for each of these rooms. The focus of each room given here is merely a suggestion. Sometimes, challenging cards will land in rooms that you associate with helpful conditions: this is when you need to look at the ambivalent meanings of the trumps. For example, when Fortitude falls in the room of the Moon, there may be an issue of being overwhelmed rather than being strong or enduring.

Threshold 0 The question or issue needing clarification. What is unknown or unrealized.

Juggler's Room 1 How you tackle the issue: the common sense or strategies you need.
Popess's Room 2 What you can learn about it. What scrutiny or silence reveal.
Empress's Room 3 What resources you bring to it. What you give or gather.
Emperor's Room 4 What authority you need to demonstrate.
Pope's Room 5 What counsel you are given about it.
Lovers' Room 6 What choice you need to make.
Chariot's Room 7 How you move forward.

Justice's Room 8 The truth you must face.
Hermit's Room 9 What you can do for yourself.
Wheel's Room 10 What changes affect it.
Fortitude's Room 11 What strengthens your position.
Hanged Man's Room 12 What is still on hold, or any betrayals.
Death's Room 13 What is coming to an end.
Temperance's Room 14 What needs adjustment or restraint.

Devil's Room 15 What is not in your interests, or any self-sabotage.
Tower's Room 16 What is collapsing or happening speedily.
Star's Room 17 What you hope for and the inspiration that the issue needs.
Moon's Room 18 What spooks or confuses you.
Sun's Room 19 What brings well-being or happiness, or which friend supports you.
Judgement's Room 20 What is coming to light. The next step.
World's Room 21 Your place in the world. How the issue plays out.

Opposite is an example of the House of Triumphs, a tableau that was read for a university graduate who asked, "Please clarify my position at this university, and how I can find a better post."

The cards drawn here are as shown. The number under each card indicates its room position in the House.

This graduate has spent a difficult first term in his rather minor post and has been thrown by his experiences so far. As we can see, his question is represented by the Fool, which is on its own position: he has come into this post with his eyes closed, we conclude. No other cards are on their own rooms, and he appears like a wide-eyed innocent. We can see his powerlessness in the middle in Room 11, where the Hanged Man is stuck in an unmoving way. I look at Room 20 to see what is coming to light: the Hermit tells us that he is only now aware of his own sloth in facing up to this situation. The poor fellow

The House of Triumphs, *Giacomo Zoni Tarot*

15	16	17	18	19	20	21
Judgement	*Star*	*Temperance*	*Wheel*	*Fortitude*	*Hermit*	*Sun*

8	9	10	11	12	13	14
Devil	*Moon*	*Juggler*	*Hanged Man*	*World*	*Emperor*	*Death*

0	1	2	3	4	5	6	7
Fool	*Chariot*	*Justice*	*Pope*	*Lovers*	*Tower*	*Empress*	*Popess*

also has Star in the room of Tower, showing that his access to hope is caving in. But something learned is something gained, in his case.

The first room he enters has the Chariot upon it: he needs to get moving and not hang about. It is clear that, with the Devil in Justice's Room 8, the truth he needs to face is that he is under extreme coercion in this post: he confirms a bullying "take it or leave it" situation, so we look at the Emperor's room, which is where the Pope has fallen. The authority he needs right now is informed and supported by some good spiritual counsel: his religion is supporting him. Looking at the room of the Hermit, he is not able to do much for himself because the Moon is there: confusion makes things too diffuse for him to act alone. The room of the Sun often shows a companion or friend and, sure enough, there is Fortitude: a strong friend who will help to give him the energy and support needed to get himself into a better place.

The World in the room of the Hanged Man, or what is still on hold, shows that this young graduate is perhaps a little slow in stepping out of his shell of academe: he is working at the same university where he studied. Happiness, in the form of the Sun on the house of the World, awaits him if he can step into the wider world. We look to the Chariot's room to see how he can move forward, and find the Popess with her book: she is the educator supreme, and it looks as if he needs to tell the world about his own academic prowess and start making some applications to other places. The Tower in the room of the Pope shows that the writing is on the wall: the university experience is gradually falling apart.

Looking at the tableau, we see that the World, Emperor and Death make a threesome: the authoritarian world which he has endured is coming to a close. He is fearful, however, of any change, as the Wheel in the room of the Moon shows. I counsel him to use discretion and a little underhand out-manoeuvring of the administration, so he can send out his job applications. He doesn't have to advertise his imminent wish for departure until it is a fait accompli! The clincher for him is the Emperor upon the house of Death: the bullying that he has endured here is definitely coming to an end. The appearance of Judgement in the Devil's room shows that his current state of entrapment is battling it out with the prospect of a renewed vision, one where his powers can be used appreciatively. The choice he needs to make now is shown in the room of the Lovers, where sits the Empress, ready to bestow and share the gifts with which he has been blessed.

After a struggle to throw off this unhappy yoke, this graduate is now happily engaged in a rewarding educational post which seems to have been tailor-made for him.

WHEN THE CARDS SPEAK

There is a point in historic tarot use, as with language learning, when arduous learning melts into fluency. First, you learn to ask the way and be polite, then you can manage basic dialogues, and finally you begin to hear, think and speak the language. Yes, you may halt and stutter sometimes, but whole sentences begin to come and you are speaking what the cards are saying. When the cards start to speak to you, you will be using your reading skills, your common sense and your instinct, as well as your vision.

For those of us who work with historic tarots, there is a strong and practical aspect to our readings. We want these older cards to speak with the accents of truth, as in the days of ancient oracles when oracular mouthpieces, the seers and visionaries, were seen as the honored servants of the truth, guiding those who governed, suffered or hoped. The position of diviner may have fallen low in our own day, but our craft must not. Reading tarot still has to be practical and answer the cutting edge of need. The wisdom of historic tarot is just as relevant and helpful to our own generation. Our practice ensures that it is properly broached, not left like undrunk antique wine, stuck in inaccessible cellars.

One of the distinctive features of any tarot is that its cards tend to depict the concerns that obtained in the era when they were made. For example, historic tarots show both the Emperor and Empress as people of importance, while folk like the Juggler don't enjoy so high a status. In our own era, we now hold showmen, actors and entertainers in high regard, while royal personages play less influential roles in our lives: for us, the Juggler paired with the Chariot might well represent the performer who wins the Best Actor award at the Oscars, for example.

While older tarots do not depict those things that we now take for granted in our society, such as electronic devices, social media or personally owned vehicles, we still have the Sun, the four Pages as the busy messengers of news, and the Chariot and 4 Batons, which can depict all of these things. Although our tarots come with medieval, Renaissance or 18th-century images upon them, we don't have to drop into those eras to make sense of the cards. No one today wants to receive a reading where the concerns of the medieval person are echoed, such as, "Your fields will be overrun by mercenaries and your family will die of plague." We all want the cards to speak to our condition, in the present time, in our own language. It is just a matter of thinking in terms of our world and opening out our vocabulary, so explore what your tarot is saying about these things.

Sometimes tarots speak clearly and formally, while at other times they can speak in colloquial slang, or with the quick riposte of two characters in a script. Although some traditional combinations will keep returning to your readings, you will also find new ones, especially when you have good questions that provoke the cards into response, when the circumstances and the cards begin to dialogue clearly. Older styles of reading are quick, fluent and immediate, revealing the untold story in a variety of pragmatic ways. But what of those things that the tarot has not yet spoken about?

Mapping the Landscape Spread

In our consideration in Chapter 1 of what a tarot is, I wrote about the way that consciousness has evolved from the collective to the individual, and how tarot has developed to answer that evolution. As citizens of the world, in a time when our global perspective is struggling with the inclusion of both individual rights and tribal needs, we all need to maintain a wider perspective in our reading to include the community viewpoint.

Over the last few decades, I have included in my divination not only the individual but also the commonwealth of the group, country or institution to which they belong. In any reading, you can look at the cards on many levels – for yourself, for your relationship with others, for the impact that events will have upon you, or the impact that you will have on your environment. As John Donne wrote, "No man is an island entire of itself"; we are part and parcel of everything, and to leave that understanding out of a divination is to fail to read the wider view. Tarot is much bigger than personal guidance. We live within a wider universe.

I created this spread in the 1980s as a map that helps us to appreciate where we are in a changing world. Around the central cross in this spread lie four other crosses, each of which contributes to your view of, and place within, the landscape. As you will see, the individual arms of the central cross also appear in one of the four other crosses.

The general positions given below can be adapted or changed for any place, person, group or event. Aspects of the topic can be assigned to this map: you might, for example, decide to assign to this map the way an election plays out in your country, or how world trends in music will influence your composition; how a year will unfold through the seasons, or how a project will develop. You can assign each cross to an aspect of your world view: the ground plan below shows how those aspects might be assigned:

Center Card Card 1 represents you in this picture, or the country, group, project or main issue.

Eastern Cross Cards 2, 7, 8, 9 represent the world of potential, origination, ideas, beginnings, things coming into being. What feeds, nourishes and grows. Preparation, unfolding, gifts. Card 6 is the core part of yourself or the issue as a family representative.

Southern Cross Cards 3, 11, 12, 13 show the world of society, group concerns, the human polity. What is transitory, fashionable or governs interest in the

Mapping the Landscape Ground Plan
*The shaded cards are at the heart of the spread and contribute to each separate cross,
serving as a reminder that they are playing parts in both the central and positional crosses.*

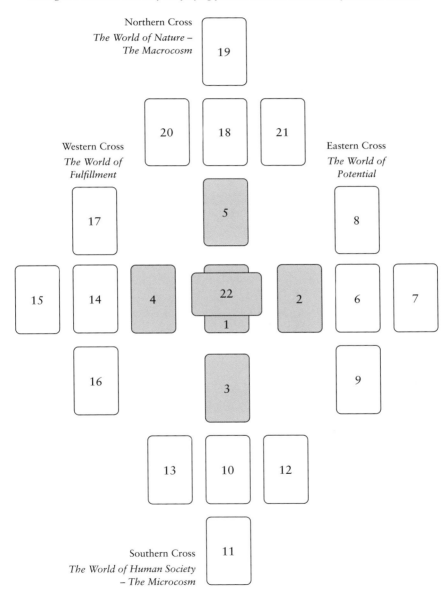

Northern Cross
*The World of Nature –
The Macrocosm*

Western Cross
*The World of
Fulfillment*

Eastern Cross
*The World of
Potential*

Southern Cross
*The World of Human Society
– The Microcosm*

present; the microcosm or the life of a people, region or country. The service that is given and embodied. Card 10 is the core part of yourself, or the issue as a representative of your tribe or society.

Western Cross Cards 4, 15, 16, 17 represent the world of fulfillment, dreams, archetypes, conclusions, things passing out of being. What matures, deepens and upholds. Card 14 is the core part of yourself or the issue as you have envisioned it into being.

Northern Cross Cards 5, 19, 20, 21 represent the world of nature, environmental influences, the world that is unseen. What is eternal and abiding, values and standards that belong to all beings; the macrocosm or the greater life of which we are all a part. The greater responsibility that is owed to the whole. Card 18 is the core part of yourself or the issue as ambassador to the universe.

Central Cross Cards 1, 2, 3, 4, 5 show your world in synthesis. Card 1 represents you or the subject of the reading. Cards 2–5 are the contributions that each of the four worlds make to your world view. Card 2: what is arising. Card 3: how human society is shaping things. Card 4: what is passing away or is still to be achieved. Card 5: the eternal view of the macrocosm.

Final Card Card 22 transcends all limitations, refusing to be restricted by the judgements or diagnoses of others. It is the gift you can use, or the warning to be aware of.

When it comes to reading each individual cross, you may also find that the cards of each cross blend together to speak eloquently. Or you might read each one like this:

- The central card is the representative of the issue.
- What is over its head is what is currently important.
- What is under its feet is what is not being noticed.
- What is to the left is the passing influence.
- What is to the right is the rising influence.

See how the central cards of each cross speak together, like a council: note how the Grand Council, made up of cards 6, 10, 14 and 18, speak with cards 1 and 22.

Mapping the Landscape of Brexit, *Playing Marseille*
Note: Spades = Swords, Clubs = Batons, Hearts = Cups, Diamonds = Deniers.

In the map on page 211, I explore how Brexit (leaving the European Union) plays out for the United Kingdom, for whom I chose the Queen of Swords as the significator.

Central Cross Ace of Swords + Queen of Swords + Wheel = the citizens of the United Kingdom make an incisive decision which puts the whole country into a whirl. Ace of Cups + 2 Cups = in supporting home issues, the country needs also to negotiate mutual exchanges once outside the EU, and to not ignore its humanitarian vision. Ace of Swords + Ace of Cups = it divides people into those who think and those who feel, riding roughshod over mutual consent.

Eastern Cross Knight of Swords + Pope = the basis for this departure stems from the appeal of British heritage and tradition. Ace of Swords + 4 Deniers = this move to self-governance will feel raw and affect the stability of the currency. Knight of Cups = attempts are made to allay intial anxiety with seductive visions of what might be.

Southern Cross

Wheel

7 Swords *World* *Empress*

2 Swords

Western Cross

Justice

10 Swords *5 Batons* *Ace of Cups*

8 Batons

Southern Cross World + Empress = the UK plays hard on the world stage to be seen as a sovereign nation. 2 Swords + 7 Swords + Wheel = British society will experience this separation as a series of setbacks and chances that will frustratingly play out over and over as deals are renegotiated.

Western Cross 5 Batons + Ace of Cups = the most important means whereby the UK can uphold its dreams is by working together in a can-do way. 8 Batons + 10 Swords + Justice = however, in order to maintain the country, a series of onerous labor laws and regulations will be enacted. 10 Swords + Ace of Cups = it is possible that the cost of maintaining the UK may be the loss of its cherished dreams. 8 Batons + Justice = strikes may result in response to these new laws.

Northern Cross Devil + 10 Cups = the wider vision shows the Devil speaking about the kind of populist democracy that enslaves rather than liberates. Knight of Batons = in response, there arises a campaigner whose sudden,

forceful action brings revolutionary change. 2 Cups + 10 Cups = there will be a new partnership that supports UK sovereignty, possibly through the Commonwealth or other allied nations, in order to maintain the national sense of our codes and beliefs. 5 Swords + 2 Cups = ethical considerations begin to address how unreciprocal things have become. 5 Swords = the UK will divorce Europe.

The presence of two Twos, two Fives and two Tens, along with three Knights, reveals that this map will unfold very rapidly indeed, with headlong speed. The only two Cups cards are 2 and 10, which speaks of great mood swings. The North East quarter has all three Knights clustered together, and I would say this represents the future candidates and generations who will pick up the pieces of this decision. The missing fourth Knight is the Knight of Deniers, showing that it is the economy that will suffer. Indeed, there is only one Denier in the whole map, which doesn't bode very well.

The central cards of each cross make this grand council:

Grand Council Queen of Swords = the UK is entering into a period of polarizing change. Pope + World = led by traditional values and focusing upon its competitive role in world markets; 5 Batons + Devil = it is facing limitation and self-delusion. The Pope, World and Devil show how issues of salvation, pragmatism and temptation combine to create short-term solutions, and also to prolong deeply polarized debates of almost religious fanaticism. The final card, the King of Batons, warns the country not to rashly exaggerate its own importance, but also offers it the gifts of courage, confidence and dynamism. If UK citizens can believe strongly enough in the possibility that this separation might succeed, there is a chance that it will. The essential flaw in the decision is the division of people into rival camps: those who see it as a nightmare and those who see regained sovereignty as the country's salvation. This energy needs to be channeled into reanimating the country, finding solutions, and maintaining its rights and safeguards.

FUTURE VOICES

If I could leave anything with you as a guide to your taromancy, then it would be to ask you to consider how these old cards might speak to people in the future. Anciently, people have divined for situations beyond themselves, asking about the wider picture – the state of a country, the best time for sowing crops, how to proceed in a time of war. Considering the times in which we live, with their economic surges, mass migrations and global business interests – not to mention world terror attacks and media-fuelled politics – whatever we divine about personally will inevitably be influenced by these factors. In my view, if we wish divination and taromancy to recover their status in our world, and not be seen as some minor footnote in history, then we will need to consider personal questions against this much wider backdrop, and to focus on the bigger picture.

I am finishing this book at a momentous time of change for my country and the world that we share. The landscape of many lives is changing beyond recognition, we can no longer see the whole view at a glance; the strategies and waymarks of the future are unclear, but these wise old cards can help us still, providing tracks whereby to map our way forward.

The tarot is a great mirror to our world, allowing us to see the landscape at one glance. Our individual lives play out on the wider stage, and the untold story that arises from the movement of the tarot cards offers us a window on how we can shape ourselves in response to these different factors. May the tarot's ancestral wisdom help us to discern the untold stories of our times for the good of all!

ENDNOTES

Please see the bibliography for full details of book titles and their publication details.

PREFACE
1 Decker, Depaulis and Dummett, p. 31ff.
2 Ibid, pp. 52–7

INTRODUCTION
3 Christian
4 Caldwell, Depaulis and Ponzi, p. 29

CHAPTER 1
5 Petrarch
6 Di Vicenzo
7 Flornoy, p. 11
8 Vitali and Zanetti, p. 25
9 Pratesi, 1989b
10 Decker, p. 31ff
11 Ben-Dov
12 Elias
13 Jodorowsky
14 Huson, pp. 30–1
15 Frati, University of Bologna ms. 4029. Caps. 119R
16 Francesco Pico della Mirandola
17 Caldwell, 2003a
18 Horodowich, p. 184
19 Caldwell, 2003b
20 Ibid
21 Frati, University of Bologna, ms. 4029. Caps. 119R
22 Vitali and Zanetti, p. 78
23 Matthews, 2013a

CHAPTER 2
24 Decker, 2013, p. 84
25 Gray
26 Leber Tarot
27 Caldwell, Depaulis and Ponzi, p. 15
28 Lévi
29 Moakley
30 Leber Tarot
31 Ibid
32 Petrarch
33 Ibid
34 Plato, Phaedrus, 253d
35 Leber Tarot

36 Ibid
37 Moakley
38 Matthews, 2004
39 Petrarch
40 Leber Tarot
41 Claudian
42 Empedocles, translated by Caítlin Matthews
43 Leber Tarot
44 Huson
45 Petrarch

CHAPTER 3
46 Mayer, 1939
47 Mayer, 1971
48 Caldwell, Depaulis and Ponzi, p. 45
49 Decker, Depaulis and Dummett, p. 72
50 Frati, p. 184
51 Jodorowsky
52 Flornoy
53 Paulmy d'Argenson, translated by Caitlín Matthews
54 Christian

CHAPTER 4
55 Cary-Yale
56 Plato, The Laws, Bk I, p. 631
57 Huson, p. 105
58 Knight
59 Ibid
60 Aristotle, II, 6

CHAPTER 5
61 Herodotus, I, 85–89
62 Matthews, 2013a
63 Ibid

CHAPTER 6
64 Ibid
65 Paulmy d'Argenson
66 Cary-Yale
67 Briggs Myers
68 Casanova, Chapter 18

CHAPTER 7
69 Pratesi, 1989a

BIBLIOGRAPHY

Aristotle, *Nichomachean Ethics*, ed. Robert C. Bartlett; Chicago: University of Chicago Press, 2012

Ben-Dov, Yoav, *Tarot: The Open Reading*; CreateSpace Independent Publishing, 2014

Berti, G. and A. Vitali, *Tarocchi Arte e Magia*; Ravenna: Edizione Le Tarot, 1994

Caldwell, Ross Sinclair, *The Devil and the Two of Hearts*; 2003a, http://www.tarotforum.net/showthread.php?t=90559

Caldwell, Ross Sinclair, *Spanish Cartomancy and Witchcraft*; 2003b, http://www.tarotforum.net/showthread.php?t=115111

Caldwell, Ross Sinclair, Thierry Depaulis & Marco Ponzi, ed. and trans. *Explaining the Tarot: Two Italian Renaissance Essays on the Meaning of the Tarot Pack*; Oxford: Maproom Publications, 2010

Cary-Yale Visconti Tarocchi Deck, ed. Stuart Kaplan; Stamford CT: US Games Systems Inc., 1984

Casanova, Giacomo, Chevalier de Seingalt, *The Complete Memoires of Casanova*; Benediction Classics, 2013

Christian, Paul (Jean-Baptiste Pitois), *Historie de la Magie, du monde surnaturel et de la fatalité à travers les temps et les peuples*, 1870, trans. by Ross Nichols as *The History and Practice of Magic*; New York: Citadel Press, 1969

Claudian, *De Raptu Proserpinae*, ed. J.B. Hall; Cambridge: Cambridge University Press, 1970

Court de Gébelin, Antoine, *Monde Primitif, analysé et comparé avec le monde modern*; 1781

Decker, Ronald, *The Esoteric Tarot: Ancient Sources Rediscovered in Hermeticism and Cabalah*; Wheaton, IL: Quest Books, 2013

Decker, Ronald, Thierry Depaulis & Michael Dummett, *A Wicked Pack of Cards*; London: Duckworth, 1996

Di Vincenzo, Sofia, *Sola Busca Tarot*; Stamford CT: US Games Systems Inc., 1998

Dummett, Michael, "Where do the Virtues Go?" in *The Playing Card*; vol. 32, no.4. 2003–4

Elias, Camelia, *Marseille Tarot: Towards the Art of Reading*; EyeCorner Press, 2013

Empedocles, *Extant Fragments*, ed. M.R. Wright; London: Bloomsbury, 2013

Flornoy, Jean-Claude, *Jean Dodal Tarot de Marseille*; Editions letarot.com, 2009

Francesco Pico della Mirandola, *De Rerum Praenotione*, 1506–7; https://archive.org/details/ioannisfrancisci00pico

Frati, L., *La vita privata di Bologna*; Bologna, 1900

Gilchrist, Cherry, *Tarot Triumphs*; Newburyport, MA: Red Wheel/Weiser, 2016

Gray, Eden, *A Complete Guide to the Tarot*; New York: Bantam Doubleday Dell, 1970

Herodotus, *The Histories*, ed. P. Cartledge; London: Penguin, 2014

Horodowich, Elizabeth, *Language and Statecraft in Early Modern Venice*; Cambridge: Cambridge University Press, 2011

Huson, Paul, *Mystical Origins of the Tarot*; Rochester VT: Destiny Books, 2004

Jodorowsky, Alejandro, *The Way of Tarot*; Rochester VT: Destiny Books, 2009

Knight, Gareth, *The Magical World of the Tarot*; York Beach, ME: Red Wheel/Weiser, 1996

Leber (Rouen) Tarot; http://trionfi.com/0/j/d/leber/

Lévi, Eliphas, *The Doctrine and Ritual of High Magic*, trans. John M. Greer; London: Tarcherperigee, 2017

McLean, Adam, "An Hermetic Origin of the Tarot Cards? A Consideration of the Tarocchi of Mantegna" in *Hermetic Journal*; London, 1983

Matthews, Caitlín, *The Complete Lenormand Oracle Handbook*; Rochester VT: Inner Traditions, 2014

Matthews, Caitlín, *The Da Vinci Enigma Tarot*; London: Connections, 2004

Matthews, Caitlín, *The One and Only Petit Etteilla Course*; www.cartomancy.net, 2013a

Matthews, Caitlín, *Sophia, Goddess of Wisdom*; Wheaton, IL: Quest Books, 2013b

Mayer, L.A., "Mamluk Playing Cards" in *Bulletin de l'Institut français d'archéologie Orientale*; Le Caire, XXXVIII, 1939, pp. 113–118

Mayer, L.A, *Mamluk Playing Cards*, ed. R. Ettinghausen and O. Kurz; Leiden, 1971

Moakley, Gertrude, *The Tarot Cards Painted by Bonifacio Bembo for the Visconti-Sforza Family*; New York: New York Public Library, 1966

Briggs Myers, Isabel, with Peter B. Myers, *Gifts Differing: Understanding Personality Type*; Mountain View, CA: Davies-Black, 1995

Paulmy d'Argenson, Marc Antoine
René de Voyer, *Mélanges Tirés
d'une Grande Bibliothèque*, Vol. 2;
Moutard, Paris, 1779

Petrarch, *The Sonnets, Triumphs
and Other Poems*; Create Space
Publishing Platform, 2016

Plato, *Complete Works*, ed. J.M.
Cooper; Indianapolis, IN: Hacklett
Publishing Co. Inc., 1997

Pollack, Rachel & Caitlín Matthews,
Tarot Tales; New York:
Ace Books, 1996

Pratesi, F., "Tarot Bolonais et
Cartomancie" in *L'As de Trèfles*,
p. 105, in *The Playing Card*, no.37,
May 1989a

Pratesi, F., "Tarot in Bologna:
documents from the University
Library" in *The Playing Card*, XVII,
no.4, 1989b, pp. 142–3

Reid, G.W., *Works of the Italian
Engravers of the Fifteenth Century*,
introduction by Bernard Quaritch,
London, 1884

Sharman-Burke, Juliet & Giovanni
Caselli, *The Sharman-Caselli Tarot
Deck*; London: Connections Book
Publishing, 2005

Vitali, Andrew & Terry Zanetti,
Il Tarocchino di Bologna; Bologna:
Edizioni Martina, 2005

TAROT USED IN THIS BOOK

All tarots were available at the time of printing.

CBD Tarot de Marseille created by Yoav Ben-Dov, www.cbdtarot.com
(permission granted by the late Yoav Ben-Dov)

Facsimile Italian Renaissance Woodcut Tarocchi by Robert Place,
https://robertmplacetarot.com/the-facsimile-italian-renaissance-woodcut-tarocchi/

Giacomo Zoni Tarot, reprinted by Il Meneghello,
http://www.arnellart.com/osvaldo/index.htm

Golden Tarot of the Renaissance (Estensi Tarot) by Giordano Berti & Jo Dworkin,
http://shop.loscarabeo.com/index.php?id_product=46&controller=
    product&id_lang=1

Minchiate Florentine, reprinted by Il Meneghello,
http://www.arnellart.com/osvaldo/index.htm

Playing Marseille by Ryan Edward, http://www.inset.cards
(Note: permission was granted to show the prototype of this deck)

Tarocchi Fine Dalla Torre in Bologna, restored by Museo Internazionale
dei Tarocchi, http://www.arnellart.com/museodeitarocchi/msdk52.htm

Tarot de Marseille Pierre Madenié 1709, restored by Yves Reynaud,
https://tarot-de-marseille-heritage.com

Vandenborre Tarot, reprinted by Lauren Forestell,
http://gameofhopelenormand.bigcartel.com

Vergnano Tarot, restored by Giordano Berti,
https://rinascimentoitalianartenglish.wordpress.com/vergnano-tarot-1830

INDEX

above and below card placement 47, 57, 69, 75, 81, 83, 85, 97, 179–81
Aces 12–13, 104, 112–13, 134–5
Adam and Eve 77
Al Leone Minchiate 142
Alexander the Great 73
Anima Mundi 87
Apollo 57, 83
Aristotle 146

Batons 14, 31, 90–93, 102–3, 128, 143
meanings of 102–27
Ben-Dov, Yoav 26, 224
blending 10, 155–7
Boccaccio 22
Bologna 23–4, 30, 75, 79

Card/s
bottom 155
colors of 153
skills 152–5
shuffling and mixing 152
sifting 190–91
speaking 206–7
turning cards face up 152
Cardinal Virtues 40, 61, 73, 108, 142–6
carte blanche 170, 190
cartiers 15, 23
cartomancy 19, 34–7
Casanova 183
CBD Tarot de Marseille 14, 16, 17, 26, 37, 48, 54, 58, 72, 86, 96, 141, 158, 180–81, 186, 188–9, 220
Chariot 22, 30, 31, 41, 43, 58–9, 88, 89, 91, 118, 207
Charlemagne, Emperor 53, 69
'Charles VI Tarot' 142–3
Christ 87
Christian, Paul 19, 93
Coins *see* Deniers

Comte de Mellet 25, 91
Conver, Nicolas 23
court cards 10, 136–49
origins of 136
remembering 139
titles of 15
Court de Gébelin 9, 25, 47, 91
Croesus of Lydi 151
Cronos 63
Cups 14–15, 31, 90–93, 102–3, 128, 143
meanings of 102–27

Dante 22
d'Argenson, Paulmy 92, 171
Death 22, 31, 41, 42, 43, 59, 70–71, 110, 114, 156, 179, 185
Dee, Jonathan 134
Deniers (Coins) 16, 31, 90–93, 102–3, 128, 144
meanings of 102–27
Devil 31, 41, 42, 43, 74–5, 89, 110, 116
directionality 35, 42, 95, 160–61, 170–82
in the courts 140–41
in the trumps 45, 47, 49, 51, 53, 55, 57, 59, 65, 73, 77, 87
divination
in retrospect 159–60
skills 150–54
Dummett, Michael 40

eagle 51, 53, 87
Edward, Ryan 26, 220
Emperor 20, 41, 43, 49, 52–3, 88, 89, 110, 114, 207
Empress 41, 43, 49, 50–51, 53, 88, 89, 110, 115, 207
Eros 57
Etteilla 25, 34–5, 55, 110, 160–61, 170

Facsimile Italian Renaissance Woodcut Tarocchi 12, 13, 22, 46,

64, 82, 133, 141, 157, 165, 220
Fool 27, 31, 41, 43, 44–45, 88, 95, 110, 207
Fortitude 18, 19, 28, 41, 43, 61, 66–7, 89, 102, 112, 142ff.
Fortuna 65
Four Last Things 85, 179
French suits 35, 90, 91–3

Geographica Tarot 24
Giacomo Zoni Tarot 15, 18, 24, 66, 76, 141, 176–7, 220
Grand Etteilla Tarot, 25, 55
Gray, Eden 45
Grimpetto, 32, 195–6
'Gringonneur Tarot' 87, 142

Hanged Man 23, 31, 32, 40, 41, 68–9, 87, 110, 113
Hermetic Order of the Golden Dawn, 25, 40, 95, 171
Hermit 22, 31, 40, 41, 43, 62–3, 88, 89, 110, 121
Hierophant *see* Pope
High Priestess *see* Popess
historic tarots
clues to reading 8–9
conciseness of 35
esoteric development of, 9, 20
folk argot of 94
landscape of 21, 32–4
language of 98, 206–7
lost skills of reading 93
meanings 30–32, 35
meanings not fixed 102
pragmatic reading of 9, 34, 90–3, 207
renaissance of 10, 21–2
skills 11
wisdom cache of 33
horse 59
Huson, Paul 83, 142

IJJ Tarot 23

Judgement 31, 41, 43, 84–5, 110, 122, 179
  known as 'the Angel' 85
Juggler 18, 28, 31, 41, 43, 46–7, 60–61, 88, 89, 95, 110, 112
Justice 17, 40, 41, 43, 59, 60–61, 102, 110, 120, 142ff., 179

Kings 15–17, 91, 127, 137ff., 145–6, 171
  meanings of 127–8
Knight, Gareth 142, 220
knighting 184, 188
Knights 15, 16, 35, 91, 93, 124–5, 137ff., 145–6, 171
  meanings of 124–5

Leber Tarot of Rouen, 45, 51, 59, 63
Levi, Eliphas 25, 47
line reading 36–7, 96–7, 158–60
lion 67, 87
Lovers 22, 28, 31, 41, 43, 53, 54–5, 88, 89, 110, 117

Ma'at 61
Magician see Juggler
major arcana see trumps
Mamluk Cards 26, 90
Mantegna Cards 20–1
Mars 59
meanings
  ambivalent 154
  by cartomantic tradition 108–28
  by number and suit 104–7
  by trumps and numbers 108–23
  learning 128
  mnemonic 111
  reversed 154
Minchiate Florentine 68, 70, 77, 109, 220
Minchiate tarots 24, 27–8, 142
minor arcana see pips

mirroring 158, 172, 189, 195
Mitelli, Guiseppe Maria 23–4, 69
Le Monde Primitif 25
Moon 22, 23, 31, 41, 43, 110, 120

Neoplatonism 20
Noblet, Jean 23
number
  increase or decrease of 153
  qualities 99–101

oracle/s
  ancient 207
  cards 26–7, 28

Pages 15, 16, 91, 92, 123–4, 137ff., 145–6, 171, 174–8, 207
  meanings of 123–4
pairing 36, 156–7
  courts 123–8
  pips 112–23
  trumps 44, 46, 48, 50, 52, 54, 56, 58, 60, 62, 64, 66, 68, 70, 72, 74, 76, 78, 80, 82, 84, 86, 88–9
Pentacles see Deniers
Persephone 75, 79
Petit Etteilla, 110, 170
Petrarch 21, 22, 55, 56, 57, 59, 63, 70, 71, 87, 88
pip cards 10–11, 19, 89–135,
  cartomantic 108–128
  features of 12–15, 98, 101
  illustrated 10, 22, 93
  multiple 130
  numbers qualities 99–101
  perceived lack of cues upon 93
Piscino, Franceso 19
Place, Robert 22, 224
Plato 58–9,142
Playing Tarot de Marseille 26, 56, 78, 132, 167, 211–14, 220
Plutus 75

Pope 18, 41, 43, 49, 54–5, 89, 110, 116
  Joan 49
  substitutions of 23, 171
Popess 18, 41, 43, 48–9, 53, 89, 110, 113
  substitutions of 23, 171
Pratesi, Franco 30–31, 96, 194,
Prudence 61, 87, 102, 142ff.
Pythagoras 99

Queens 15, 16, 91, 125–6, 137ff., 145–6, 171
  meanings of 125–6
questions 9, 128, 130, 150–51, 156, 162
  create apertures 34, 150

reading
  by the Cardinal Virtues 95
  by cartomantic tradition 95, 108–28
  by common sense 34
  by court and suit 137
  by direction 95
  by eye 30–32, 35, 36, 95, 96–8
  by foliage on pips 98
  by functions of the body 95, 108
  by number and suit, 35, 95, 104–7
  by number and trump 95, 108–23
  by suggestive features 33–4
  dogmatism in 98
  numbers as indicators in 94–5
  on collective and community issues 208–15
  third-party 185, 195
regional tarot patterns 23
  Bolognese 23–4, 40–41
  Ferrarese 21–2, 40–41
  Milanese 40–41,
Renaud, Yves 23
reversals 25, 42, 111, 154
Rider Waite-Smith Tarot 8,

10, 22, 25, 83, 93, 178
Roman numerals 11
Rosenwald Minchiate Tarot
  87

Saturn 21, 142
Sharman-Caselli Tarot 94, 95
significators 148, 149,
  170–72, 173–5, 183ff.,
  190, 198–9
Smith, Pamela Coleman, 25,
  95
Sola Busca 22
Spades 94
Spreads
  Arch of Nine 191
  Building the Story from
    the Gaze 179–82
  Cross and Passport 164–6
  De Mellet's Pips 131–2
  Finding the Way 197–201
  Fountain Spread 168–9
  Four Aces Spread 134
  Grimpetto's Spread 195–7
  House of Triumphs 202–6
  How are they hiring?
    158–9
  Is he reliable? 154–5
  Line and Leader 191
  Line of Cardea and Janus
    162–3
  Lines 36–7, 155
  Lost Card 96–7
  Mapping the Landscape
    Spread 208–15
  Messengers of News
    174–8
  Mirror Pairs 172–3
  Pole of Balance 191
  Pyramid Spread 166–8
  Sir Thomas More's Trial
    159–60
  Tableau of Twenty-five
    183–90
  Three-card Layer 133–4
  What's wrong with the
    TV? 162–3
  Where Two Courts Meet
    147–9

Why is my partner
    annoying me? 130
Star 22, 23, 30, 41, 43, 46,
  78, 89, 110, 118
Strength *see* Fortitude
suits 13–16, 137
  common significance 91,
    92–3
  esoteric significance 91
  interactions 129–30, 201
  long and round, 24, 92
  origins 90–3
  qualities of 102–3
Sun 31, 41, 42, 43, 82–3,
  88, 89, 121, 179, 207
Swords 13, 31, 90–3,
  102–3, 128, 143
  meanings of 102–27

Tableau reading 36, 182–93
Tarocchi Fine Dalla Torre
  141, 163, 195, 220
Tarocchino Bolognese 23,
  30–32, 36, 83, 96
  methods of reading 89,
    173–4, 194–201
tarot
  Appropriati 8, 28
  choosing a 19, 220
  esoteric 25, 91
  fortune-telling with 20, 28
  future of 207, 215
  gambling with 20, 25,
    26ff., 194
  Gypsies and Egyptians
    falsely seen as
    originators of 25, 93
  origins of 21–2, 25, 34,
    90–3
  prohibitions against 26,
    28–9
  psychological 178–9
  purpose of 20–21
  spellcraft with 20, 75
  taxes on 23
Tarot de Besançon 23
Tarot de Marseilles 8, 17,
  19, 22, 23, 24, 35, 40, 42,
  65, 95, 98, 143, 178, 179

variant types of 57
*Tarot de Marseille Pierre
  Madenié* 12, 16, 23, 44,
  50, 52, 94, 97, 172, 220
Tarot de Paris, 22, 49
tarotmancer 8, 19, 32, 34,
  171
Temperance 30, 31, 41, 43,
  61, 72–3, 102, 110, 115,
  142ff.
tetraktys 99
Themis 61
Tower 22, 28, 41, 43, 76–7,
  88, 89, 110, 117
I Trionfi 21–2, 55, 56, 57,
  59, 63, 86, 87
trumps or triumphs 10, 19,
  38–89
  as indicators of time,
    motion, pace 88
  forward-facing 42, 60, 68,
    75, 83, 85, 178–202
  iconography of 38–9
  sequential pairings of 88–9

Vandenborre Tarot 23, 29,
  60, 74, 156, 174–5, 220
Venus 79
Vera Sibilla 111
Viéville Tarot 23, 79
Vergano Tarot 17, 24, 62,
  80, 84, 155, 220
Visconti family 10, 49
Visconti Tarots 22, 65, 67,
  87, 171

Waite, A.E. 25
Wands *see* Batons
Wheel of Fortune 28, 41,
  43, 63, 64–5, 88, 89, 91,
  110, 122, 142
  as suit and meaning
    indicator 108–9
Wirth, Oswald 25
World 22, 27, 31, 41, 43,
  86, 88, 89, 110, 112,
  142–3

Zeus 57

ABOUT THE AUTHOR

Caitlín Matthews' books, courses and events may be seen at:
www.hallowquest.org.uk
Her divination and myth blog is http://caitlin-matthews.blogspot.co.uk

ACKNOWLEDGEMENTS

I would like first to acknowledge the generosity of deck creators and tarot restorers who have kindly granted permission to use their images, enabling this book to be illustrated so beautifully: to the late Yoav Ben-Dov, and to Giordano Berti, Morena Poltronieri of the Museo de Tarot, Tag Jorrit, Robert Place, Yves Renaud, Osvaldo Menegazzi and Cristina Dorsini at Il Meneghello in Milan, Lo Scarabeo, and lastly to Ryan Edward – your craft rings the world in beauty!

I give reverence to my teachers, Dolores Ashcroft-Nowicki and Gareth Knight, and applaud my colleagues R.J. Stewart, Alison Cross, Andrea Aste, Rachel Pollack, Mary Greer and all with whom I work in the tarot world, whose visions and dialogues keep us young. I thank those who have kindly allowed me to present some of my ideas in this book at their conferences: Kim Arnold of the UK Tarot Conference in London, Linda Henery of the Tarot Guild of Australia, and Wald and Ruth Amberson of the Reader's Studio in New York. Thanks to all tarot scholars whose combined researches have made this book possible: you are graven in the halls of memory! To those clients who allowed their readings to be used here, with changes of details and names, I bless you for agreeing to share your predicaments and questions so that others might learn.

Thanks to John for putting up with tarot cards littering every surface of our house, and to Nick, Stephane and all at Eddison Books for bringing the book to light. Thanks to Jane Struthers for expert editing. Lastly, to my cat, Willow, who remains the inscrutable White Lady of Tarot, whose delicate paws, nose and tail have chosen many a card: thank you for your exquisite forbearance.